AIR FRYER COOKBOOK FOR BEGINNERS

Your Complete Guide For Beginners to Bake, Grill and Roast Delicious Daily Recipes!

Joanne Broadhurst

Table of Contents

Introduction 6
Chapter 1. Introduction About the Air Fryer 7
   How Does the Air Fryer Work? 7
   How To Clean the Air Fryer 8
Chapter 2. Differences Between an Air Fryer and A Classic Fryer 9
Chapter 3. Air Fryer Tips & Tricks 10
Chapter 4. BREAKFAST RECIPES 11
   1. Italian Frittata 11
   2. Mushroom Scrambled Eggs 11
   3. Sage and Pear Sausage Patties 12
   4. Nutty French Toast 12
   5. Cottage Cheesy Pancakes 13
   6. Nut and Berry Granola 13
   7. Breakfast Monkey Bread 14
   8. Crustless Mini Quiches 14
   9. Herbed Vegetable Breakfast Bake 15
   10. Baked Eggs in Tomato Sauce 15
   11. Pesto Omelet 16
   12. Cranberry Oatmeal Muffins 17
   13. Raspberry-Stuffed French Toast 17
   14. Tofu Scramble Bowls 18
   15. Peaches and Cream Oatmeal Bake 18
Chapter 5. POULTRY RECIPES 20
   16. Curried Chicken Nuggets 20
   17. Chicken Fajitas 20
   18. Orange Chicken and Snap Peas 21
   19. Chicken Parm Hoagies 22
   20. Stir-Fried Chicken with Pineapple 22
   21. Chicken Casserole 23
   22. Chicken Satay 24
   23. Balsamic Roasted Chicken Thighs 24
   24. Mini Turkey Meatloaves 25
   25. Tex-Mex Turkey Burgers 25
   26. Turkey Spinach Meatballs 26

27.	Cranberry Turkey Quesadillas	26
28.	Turkey–Stuffed Zucchini Boats	27
29.	Turkey-Stuffed Bell Peppers	27
30.	Breaded Turkey Cutlets	28

Chapter 6. BEEF, PORK, AND LAMB RECIPES 29

31.	Steak Bites and Mushrooms	29
32.	Mongolian Beef	29
33.	Stir-Fried Steak and Cabbage	30
34.	Beef Tips and Gravy	30
35.	Garlic-Herb Rib Eye	31
36.	Pork Belly Bites	31
37.	Sweet-and-Sour Polish Sausage	32
38.	Honey-Garlic Pork Chops	32
39.	Pork Medallions in Mustard Sauce	33
40.	Lemon Pork Tenderloin	34
41.	Mustard Lamb Chops	34
42.	Savory Lamb Chops	35
43.	Herbed Lamb Steaks	35
44.	Air Fryer Lamb Meatballs	36
45.	Rosemary Lamb Chops	36

Chapter 7. FISH AND SEAFOOD RECIPES 37

46.	California Fish Tacos	37
47.	Cilantro Butter Baked Mahi Mahi	37
48.	Honey-Balsamic Salmon	38
49.	Sriracha Tuna Melt	38
50.	Baked Chili-Lime Tilapia	39
51.	Garlic-Dill Salmon with Tomatoes	39
52.	Lemon-Herb Tuna Steaks	40
53.	Parmesan Garlic Shrimp	41
54.	Lemony Sea Scallops	41
55.	Crispy Calamari	42
56.	Shrimp and Crab Cakes	42

Chapter 8. SIDE DISHES 44

| 57. | Roasted Spicy Corn | 44 |

58.	Crispy Mushrooms	44
59.	Roasted Carrots	45
60.	Parmesan Asparagus	45
61.	Five-Spice Broccoli	46
62.	Caramelized Sweet Potatoes	46
63.	Roasted Italian Bell Peppers	47

Chapter 9.   VEGAN RECIPES 48
64.	Chili-Lime Bean and Rice Burritos	48
65.	Roasted Garlic Brussels Sprouts	48
66.	Garlicky Green Beans	49
67.	Steamed Green Veggie Trio	49
68.	Roasted Waldorf Salad	50
69.	Stir-Fried Zucchini and Yellow Squash	50
70.	Crispy Fried Okra	51
71.	Herbed Vegetable Mélange	51
72.	Crispy Ginger Edamame	52
73.	Roasted Cherry Tomatoes	52

Chapter 10.   APPETIZERS RECIPES 54
74.	Jalapeño Poppers	54
75.	Spinach-Cranberry Turnovers	54
76.	Apricots in Blankets	55
77.	Tex-Mex Cheese Sticks	56
78.	Buffalo Cauliflower Bites	56
79.	Tandoori-Style Chickpeas	57
80.	Roasted Garlic and Onion Dip	57

Chapter 11.   SNACK RECIPES 59
81.	Cajun-Spiced Roasted Pecans	59
82.	Crispy Sweet Potato Fries	59
83.	Radish Chips	60
84.	Brie and Bacon Mini Tartlets	60
85.	Crispy French Fries	61
86.	Bruschetta Basil Pesto	61
87.	Air Fryer Popcorn	62
88.	Soda Bread Currant Muffins	62

- 89. Cheesy Corn Bread 63
- 90. Banana-Walnut Bread 63

Chapter 12. DESSERT RECIPES 65

- 91. Pound Cake Bites with Cinnamon Dip 65
- 92. Chocolate Chunk Cookies 65
- 93. Grilled Curried Fruit 66
- 94. Pistachio Baked Pears 66
- 95. Cracker Candy 67
- 96. Apple Peach Cranberry Crisp 67
- 97. Peanut Butter Brownies 68
- 98. Carrot Cake Muffins 68
- 99. Mini Baked Apple Pies 69
- 100. Chewy Date Bars 70

RECIPE INDEX 71
AIR FRYER TIME TABLE 75
COOKING CONVERSION CHART 80
Conclusion 81

Introduction

When you think of clean eating, fried food may not be the first thing to come to mind. But the truth is that there is a huge misconception regarding what air fryers can do. They do more than just heat up frozen foods that would normally be deep-fried!

This versatile appliance can also be used for baking, roasting, reheating, dehydrating, and grilling. There are even air fryer units that have a rotisserie attachment. This means you can make a variety of foods without using extra oil, with the bonus of reduced cook times. The air fryer can help you achieve all sorts of textures and flavors in food that might otherwise not be possible. And by eliminating unhealthy oils often used in cooking, you can add some of your favorite foods back onto your menu.

In this cookbook, you will find an extensive collection of beginner-friendly recipes designed to showcase the versatility of your air fryer. From classic favorites like chicken wings and French fries to more unexpected dishes like meatballs and seafood, this cookbook offers something for everyone. Best of all, each recipe features easy-to-follow instructions and ingredients that are both healthy and delicious. Whether you are new to air frying or a seasoned pro, the Air Fryer Cookbook for Beginners is sure to become a go-to resource for easy and satisfying meals.

Chapter 1. Introduction About the Air Fryer

Air fryers were originally introduced in the early 2010s and were a hit among foodies seeking a healthier way to fry their favorite foods. The first patent on this type of cooking device is credited to a company called Philips Electronics, which released its first air fryer in Europe in 2010.

The popularity of air fryers continued to grow as people began to recognize the health benefits and convenience of this low-fat alternative to traditional frying. Brands such as Ninja, Farberware, and Cuisinart entered the market with their own versions of air fryers, each with unique features to further improve the cooking experience. The technology behind this innovative gadget uses a high-powered fan and heating elements to create the illusion of frying while cooking with hot air instead of oil. It's not surprising that today air fryers have become a staple in the modern kitchen.

Today, air fryers can now be found all over the globe and are being used neatly in every household. With healthier alternative kitchen appliances increasing in popularity, it's only a matter of time before more innovations hit the market. What started as a small niche appliance has now become a kitchen must-have for health-conscious consumers everywhere.

With new advancements in air frying technology and more companies releasing their own versions of the appliance, there's no doubt that the air fryer is here to stay.

How Does the Air Fryer Work?

The air fryer is a small countertop kitchen appliance designed to cook foods faster and with limited or no additional oil. Most compared to a convection oven, an air fryer uses an electric heating element to circulate hot air around the foods to cook them. Air fryers can reach up to 445°F depending upon the model.

This allows your food to crisp well without the use of oil. It also makes cooking time shorter than it would be in a traditional oven. This saves you time in the kitchen and helps you maintain the basic parameters of clean eating with ease.

Whether you have a basket-style air fryer or one with racks or grilling options, it can do many of the same kinds of cooking as a deep fryer, an oven, or even your stove top.

Roasting and frying in the air fryer are ideal for keeping cuts of meat moist on the inside and crispy on the outside. If a grilling rack is included with your fryer, you'll find grilled foods are quicker to make and require less cleanup than traditional grilling.

Finally, the fryer can be used for baking and can even make low-oil stir-fries.

How To Clean the Air Fryer

The manual that came with your air fryer will discuss how to clean and care for it. It is important to read this carefully and follow the instructions, as that will help to keep your air fryer in optimum condition. Each air fryer is a little different, so it is best to pay special attention to the cleaning instructions of the air fryer model that you have.

Often, cleaning can be done with a damp cloth or wet wipes but be sure to check if any special cleaning materials are required. Additionally, take some time to check for any damages on the appliance, such as frayed cords or loose parts, and handle them with care to avoid any unnecessary accidents.

It is always a good idea to read the manual in full and check for any recalls that apply to your model just to stay up to date with the best maintenance practices. Lastly, do not forget to inspect the appliance before use; this will help you to ensure that you are using it in the safest way and that it is operating at its peak performance level.

Chapter 2. Differences Between an Air Fryer and A Classic Fryer

Fried foods are a delight, but it's widely known that the risk of heart disease and other health problems increases with frequent consumption of oily and fatty foods. However, thanks to technological innovations, we have a plethora of options that give us the indulgence to eat fried food without compromising our health. Two of these alternatives are classic fryers and air fryers. Although they achieve similar results, their methods are entirely different, and they have distinctive features to offer.

One of the primary differences between an air fryer and a classic fryer is the cooking technique. A traditional fryer relies on submerged oil to fry up food, while air fryers use hot air to give food that crispy texture. Another significant difference is that air fryers are less messy than classic fryers, making them an ideal cooking solution for those who want to avoid all the hassle that comes with cleaning up after frying food.

In contrast, with classic fryers, consistent monitoring is required to prevent spillovers, which can be considerable, from spreading out and causing the surrounding area to become oily. However, in the case of an air fryer, this mess is easily avoided because there is no oil involved to splatter about. This advantage makes air fryers an excellent choice for people with busy lifestyles who don't have much time to spend cleaning up the kitchen.

Moreover, since air fryers don't use oil, they are considered healthier than traditional fryers since they cut down on fat intake while achieving the same golden color and crispy texture. Furthermore, using an air fryer also means that you can avoid the lingering smell of stale oil in your kitchen, as well as the discomfort and extra cleaning that comes with using a classic fryer.

Another benefit of air fryers is that they are more versatile than traditional fryers. These appliances can be used to not only fry but also grill, roast, and bake foods, which adds to their convenience and versatility in the kitchen. In conclusion, while both classic and air fryers have their advantages, choosing an air fryer means healthier eats, less mess to worry about, and more flexibility in the kitchen.

Chapter 3. Air Fryer Tips & Tricks

When it comes to getting the most out of your air fryer, there are a few tips worth keeping in mind.

1. First, it's important to follow the directions that come with the air fryer to ensure you use it correctly.

2. Make sure to preheat the air fryer for at least three minutes before adding the ingredients. This helps to ensure that the food cooks evenly and thoroughly.

3. It's important to cut the ingredients into smaller pieces. Spread them out in one layer to ensure that they all cook evenly and don't burn or dry out.

4. Try pre-coating the ingredients with oil before adding them to the air fryer basket. This helps to ensure that the food does not stick to the surface and gives it a crispier finish.

5. Be sure to shake the air fryer basket a few times during the cooking process to ensure that the ingredients are cooked evenly and thoroughly.

6. Never overfill the air fryer as it can make it difficult for the hot air to circulate and the food won't cook evenly.

7. Use caution when removing foods or opening the fryer lid to prevent burns from the hot air and steam.

8. After taking the food out of the air fryer, let it sit until it cools down. This will help to lock in the moisture and ensure that the food is cooked to the desired degree or texture.

9. To ensure that the air fryer does its job correctly, clean the basket and fryer regularly. This helps to prevent the accumulation of grease and oils and keeps the internal components of the air fryer running smoothly.

10. Lastly, it's also important to check your air fryer for any loose parts or cracks that could potentially create a hazard.

Chapter 4. BREAKFAST RECIPES

1. Italian Frittata

Prep time: 10 mins | Cook time: 12 mins | Serves: 3

ING:

- one tbs. unsalted butter, at room temperature
- 4 large eggs, beaten
- ¼ c. ricotta cheese
- ¼ c. whole milk
- 1 t. dried Italian seasoning
- Pinch sea salt
- 2 scallions, chopped
- 1 minced clove garlic
- One-third c. chopped cherry tomatoes, drained
- ½ c. provolone cheese, shredded
- ¼ c. Parmesan cheese, grated

Instructions:

1. Oil your 7" circle dish with butter, then put aside.
2. In your med. dish, whisk eggs, ricotta, milk, Italian seasoning, and salt. Pour this into the prepared pan.
3. Arrange the scallions, garlic, and tomatoes on the eggs. Top with the cheeses.
4. Set your air fryer to 350°Fahrenheit. Put your dish in your basket and cook for 12 mins. Serve.

Nutritional Values: Calories: 285; Fat: 21g; Carbs: 5g; Protein: 21g

2. Mushroom Scrambled Eggs

Prep time: 10 mins | Cook time: 14 mins | Serves: 3

ING:

- two tbs. butter
- ⅔ c. sliced mushrooms
- one scallion, chopped
- 6 eggs, big
- two tbs. cream, light
- one-half t. each of dried thyme & sea salt
- ground black pepper

Instructions:

1. Warm up your air fryer to 350° Fahrenheit.
2. Place butter in your 6-x-2" circle dish and put it in your cooking basket. Melt butter within 1 min.

3. Remove the basket and put mushrooms and scallions to your pan. Return your basket and bake for 5 mins, shaking after 3 mins.
4. Meanwhile, in your med. dish, whisk eggs, cream, thyme, salt, plus pepper until combined.
5. Remove air fryer basket and pour the egg mixture into your pan. Bake again for 8 mins, mixing after five mins. Serve.

Nutritional Values: Calories: 246; Fat: 21g; Carbs: 2g; Protein: 14g

3. Sage and Pear Sausage Patties

Prep time: 15 mins | Cook time: 15 mins | Serves: 6

ING:

- one pound pork, ground
- one-fourth cup pear, chopped
- one tbsp sage leaves, chopped
- one clove garlic, minced
- one-half t. sea salt
- ground black pepper

Instructions:

1. In your med. dish, mix all the fixings, and form it into patties.
2. Warm up your air fryer to 375°Fahrenheit. Put patties in your basket, and air fry for fifteen mins, turning once. Serve.

Nutritional Values: Calories: 204; Fat: 16g; Carbs: 1g; Protein: 13g

4. Nutty French Toast

Prep time: 15 mins | Cook time: 7 mins | Serves: 4

ING:

- 2 large eggs
- ⅔ c. whole milk
- one t. vanilla
- 4 slices French bread
- ⅓ c. brown sugar, packed
- One-fourth c. butter
- ⅔ c. pecans, chopped
- ¼ t. cinnamon

Instructions:

1. In a big, shallow dish, mix milk, eggs, add vanilla until smooth.
2. Place bread slices into your dish and let sit. Flip bread and allow it to sit until you're ready to cook.
3. In your small pan over low temperature, combine brown sugar and butter, stirring occasionally until dissolved.
4. In your small dish, toss pecans and cinnamon.

5. Put bread slices in your basket. Drizzle brown sugar mixture over the bread and top with the pecans.
   6. Set your air fryer to 350°Fahrenheit. Bake for 7 minutes till the French toast is golden brown and crisp. Serve.

Nutritional Values: Calories: 475; Fat: 31g; Carbs: 41g; Protein: 11g

5. Cottage Cheesy Pancakes

Prep time: 15 mins | Cook time: 13 mins | Serves: 3

ING:

- ¼ c. flour, all-purpose
- one tbs. sugar, granulated
- ¼ t. baking powder
- Two big eggs
- ¼ c. 2% milk
- ¼ c. small curd cottage cheese
- Two tbs. each of vegetable oil, butter & brown sugar
- one apple, sliced ⅛" thick
- ½ t. cinnamon

Instructions:

1. In your med. dish, mix flour, sugar, and baking powder.
2. In your 2-cup dish, whisk milk, eggs, cottage cheese, and oil till blended.
3. Mix both mixture and let stand while you prepare the apple mixture.
4. Warm up your air fryer to 375°Fahrenheit. Put butter in your 6-x-2" circle dish, place it in your basket, cook within one min and remove.
5. Top evenly with the brown sugar, apples, plus cinnamon. Bake this mixture within 3 mins till butter bubbles. Remove the dish.
6. Pour the batter over the apples. Bake again within 9 mins till golden brown. Serve.

Nutritional Values: Calories: 341; Fat: 21g; Carbs: 31g; Protein: 9g

6. Nut and Berry Granola

Prep time: 15 mins | Cook time: 12 mins | Serves: 6

ING:

- One & half c. rolled oats
- One c. pecans or walnuts, chopped
- 3 tbs. flaxseed
- One-half t. cinnamon
- One-eight t. nutmeg
- One-fourth c. maple syrup
- 3 tbs. vegetable oil
- One t. vanilla
- One-fourth t. sea salt

- One-half c. dried blueberries
- One-half c. dried cherries

Instructions:

1. In your big dish, mix oats, nuts, flaxseed, cinnamon, and nutmeg.
2. In your 2-cup dish, mix maple, oil, vanilla, and salt. Stir it with the oat mixture, then put in your 7" circle dish.
3. Warm up your air fryer to 350°Fahrenheit. Put dish in your basket and bake for twelve mins, stirring once.
4. Move it to your serving dish, then cool for 3 mins. Mix in dried blueberries and cherries. Let it stand until cool, then serve.

Nutritional Values: Calories: 361; Fat: 21g; Carbs: 38g; Protein: 6g

7. Breakfast Monkey Bread

Prep time: 5 mins | Cook time: 6 mins | Serves: 4

ING:

- 8 ounces canned biscuits, refrigerated, cut each biscuit into four
- ¼ c. sugar, white
- three tbs. sugar, brown
- ½ t. cinnamon
- ⅛ t. nutmeg
- three tbs. no-salt butter, dissolved

Instructions:

1. Mix all ingredients except biscuits and butter in your deep dish.
2. Soak each biscuit into your butter, then coat it in your prepared mixture. Move them in your 6-x-6-x-2" air fryer-safe cooking dish.
3. Bake for six mins till golden, cool for 5 mins, and serve.

Nutritional Values: Calories: 393; Fat: 17g; Carbs: 55g; Protein: 5g

8. Crustless Mini Quiches

Prep time: 10 mins | Cook time: 15 mins | Serves: 3

ING:

- Six big eggs
- One-fourth c. sour cream
- one tbs. cornstarch
- One-half c. hash brown potatoes, shredded
- One-half c. each of shredded Swiss cheese & Colby cheese
- one minced scallion
- one tbs. minced chives

Instructions:

1. Place 6 silicone muffin cups in your cooking basket. Put aside.
2. In your big dish, whisk eggs, sour cream, and cornstarch.
3. Put potatoes, Swiss and Colby cheeses, scallion, and chives and mix well.
4. Using a ¼-cup measure, divide the mixture among the muffin cups in your basket.
5. Warm up your air fryer to 325°Fahrenheit. Bake for 15 mins till golden brown. Serve.

Nutritional Values: Calories: 382; Fat: 27g; Carbs: 11g; Protein: 23g

9. Herbed Vegetable Breakfast Bake

Prep time: 10 mins | Cook time: 18 mins | Serves: 4

ING:

- oil spray
- 6 eggs
- ½ yellow onion, diced
- ½ c. diced mushrooms
- two tbs. chopped parsley
- one tbs. chopped chives, + more for garnish
- ½ tbs. chopped dill
- ½ c. grated Gruyère cheese

Instructions:

1. Warm up your air fryer to 350°Fahrenheit. Spray your 6-inch baking dish using oil. Set aside.
2. In your med. dish, whisk eggs, onion, mushrooms, parsley, chives, dill, and Gruyère cheese.
3. Move it into your baking dish and bake in your air fryer for 18 mins till eggs are set in the center.
4. Serve immediately with additional chives over the top.

Nutritional Values: Calories: 167; Fat: 11g; Carbs: 3g; Protein: 14g

10. Baked Eggs in Tomato Sauce

Prep time: 10 mins | Cook time: 10 mins | Serves: 4

ING:

- oil spray
- 2 tbs. tomato paste
- ½ c. low-sodium chicken broth
- 4 Roma tomatoes, diced
- 2 garlic cloves, minced
- ½ t. oregano, dried
- ½ t. basil, dried
- One-fourth t. each of red pepper flakes & paprika, salt & ground black pepper
- four eggs

- two scallions, diced
- one c. grated cheddar cheese

Instructions:

1. Set your air fryer to 350°Fahrenheit. Oil four 6-ounce ramekins. Put aside.
2. In your big dish, mix the tomato paste, broth, tomatoes, garlic, oregano, basil, pepper flakes, and paprika until combined.
3. Put mixture into your ramekins and bake for 5 mins. Remove, and crack single egg into each ramekin.
4. Sprinkle using salt, pepper, scallions plus grated cheese. Cook again for another 3 mins till cheese melted. Serve immediately.

Nutritional Values: Calories: 300; Fat: 16g; Carbs: 22g; Protein: 1+g

11. Pesto Omelet

Prep time: 10 mins | Cook time: 13 mins | Serves: 3

ING:

- one tbs. olive oil
- one shallot, minced
- one clove garlic, minced
- one-half c. red bell pepper, diced
- one-fourth c. chopped fresh tomato
- 4 large eggs
- 2 tbs. light cream
- ¼ t. sea salt
- ½ c. shredded mozzarella cheese
- 3 tbs. basil pesto

Instructions:

1. In your 6" round dish, toss oil, shallot, garlic, bell pepper, and tomato.
2. Set your air fryer to 350°Fahrenheit. Put your pan dish in your basket and cook for 3 mins, stirring once, until veggies are tender.
3. Meanwhile, mix eggs, cream, and salt in your small dish.
4. When vegetables are done, remove the basket, add egg mixture, and cook for 8 mins.
5. Sprinkle with cheese, then cook again within 2 minutes till eggs are set. Top with the pesto and serve immediately.

Nutritional Values: Calories: 308; Fat: 25g; Carbs: 8g; Protein: 15g

12. Cranberry Oatmeal Muffins

Prep time: 15 mins | Cook time: 12 mins | Serves: 4

ING:

- ½ c. flour, all-purpose
- 2 tbs. flour, whole-wheat
- ½ t. baking powder
- two tbs. brown sugar
- three tbs. quick-cooking oats
- Pinch sea salt
- one big egg
- one-fourth c. whole milk
- one t. vanilla
- 2 tbs. vegetable oil
- ⅓ c. dried cranberries
- Nonstick baking spray containing flour

Instructions:

1. In a med. dish, combine all dry ingredients. In your small dish, beat all wet ingredients. Combine both mixtures, then stir in the cranberries.
2. Spray four silicone muffin cups with the baking spray. Divide the batter among them, filling each two-thirds full.
3. Warm up air fryer to 325°Fahrenheit. Put muffin cups in your basket and bake for 12 mins till the muffins are browned.

Nutritional Values: Calories: 232; Fat: 9g; Carbs: 32g; Protein: 5g

13. Raspberry-Stuffed French Toast

Prep time: 15 mins | Cook time: 8 mins | Serves: 4

ING:

- four (one" thick) French bread slices
- 2 tbs. raspberry jam
- ⅓ c. fresh raspberries
- 2 egg yolks
- ⅓ c. 2% milk
- 1 tbs. sugar
- ½ t. vanilla extract
- 3 tbs. sour cream

Instructions:

1. Slice a pocket into each bread slice, making sure you don't cut through to the other side.
2. In your small dish, mix raspberry jam and raspberries, crushing raspberries into the jam with a fork.

3. In your shallow dish, whisk egg yolks with the sugar, milk, and vanilla until combined.
4. Put sour cream in the pocket you cut in the bread slices, then add the raspberry mixture. Squeeze the edges of the bread slightly to close the opening.
5. Soak bread in your egg mixture and allow to stand for 3 mins. Turn bread and stand for 3 mins.
6. Set your air fryer to 375°Fahrenheit. Arrange stuffed bread in your basket.
7. Air fry for 5 mins, flip bread slices and cook again for 3 mins, until the French toast is golden brown.

Nutritional Values: Calories: 278; Fat: 6g; Carbs: 46g; Protein: 9g

14. Tofu Scramble Bowls

Prep time: 10 mins | Cook time: 15 mins | Serves: 2

ING:

- one med. russet potato, slice into fries
- one bell pepper, remove & slice into 1" strips
- ½ (14-ounce) block moderate-firm tofu, drained & cubed
- one tbs. nutritional yeast
- ½ t. each of garlic & onion, granulated
- One-fourth t. turmeric, ground
- one tbs. apple cider vinegar

Instructions:

1. Place the potato and pepper strips in your cooking basket or on the rack and fry at 400°Fahrenheit for 10 mins.
2. Meanwhile, in a small pan, combine tofu, nutritional yeast, granulated garlic, granulated onion, turmeric, and apple cider vinegar.
3. Put pan into your air fryer, on a rack above the potatoes and peppers. Continue to fry at 400°F for 5 mins till potatoes are crispy and tofu is heated through.
4. Remove pan and stir with tofu. Divide the potatoes and peppers evenly between 2 bowls. Then spoon half the tofu over each bowl. Serve warm.

Nutritional Values: Calories: 267; Fat: 6g; Carbs: 42g; Protein: 15g

15. Peaches and Cream Oatmeal Bake

Prep time: 5 mins | Cook time: 8 mins | Serves: 4

ING:

- oil spray
- two c. old-fashioned rolled oats
- ½ t. baking powder
- One & half t. ground cinnamon
- ⅛ t. salt
- One & one-fourth c. unsweetened vanilla almond milk
- ¼ c. maple syrup
- one t. vanilla extract
- two peaches, peeled & diced, divided

Instructions:

1. Warm up your air fryer to 350°Fahrenheit. Oil four 6-ounce ramekins using olive oil. Put aside.
2. In your big dish, combine all dry ingredients. Mix in milk, maple, vanilla, plus three-quarters of the diced peaches.
3. Move mixture into your ramekins and bake for 8 mins till golden. Serve with diced peaches on top.

Nutritional Values: Calories: 256; Fat: 4g; Carbs: 50g; Protein: 8g

Chapter 5. POULTRY RECIPES

16. Curried Chicken Nuggets

Prep time: 10 mins | Cook time: 7 mins | Serves: 4

ING:

- One lb. no bones & skin chicken breasts, sliced into 1" pieces
- four t. curry powder
- one-half t. sea salt
- one-eight t. ground black pepper
- one egg, beaten
- two tbs. butter, melted
- one c. panko breadcrumbs
- oil spray
- ½ c. plain Greek yogurt
- ⅓ c. mango chutney
- ¼ c. mayonnaise

Instructions:

1. Sprinkle the chicken pieces with 3 teaspoons of curry powder, salt, and pepper; toss to coat.
2. In your shallow dish, beat egg and melted butter. Put breadcrumbs on your plate.
3. Dip chicken in your egg mixture, then coat with breadcrumbs. Put coated nuggets on a wire rack as you work.
4. Warm up air fryer to 400°Fahrenheit. Put nuggets in your basket, mist with cooking oil, and cook for 7 minutes, tossing once.
5. Repeat with remaining half of chicken nuggets.
6. Meanwhile, in your small dish, mix yogurt, chutney, mayo, plus remaining curry powder. Serve the nuggets with the dipping sauce.

Nutritional Values: Calories: 426; Fat: 22g; Carbs: 24g; Protein: 32g

17. Chicken Fajitas

Prep time: 10 mins | Cook time: 10 mins | Serves: 4

ING:

- 4 no bones & skin sliced chicken breasts
- one small sliced red onion
- two sliced red bell peppers
- ½ c. spicy ranch salad dressing, divided
- ½ t. dried oregano
- 8 corn tortillas
- two c. torn butter lettuce
- two avocados, peeled & chopped

Instructions:
1. Put chicken, onion, and pepper in your cooking basket. Toss 1 tablespoon salad dressing and oregano.
2. Grill for 10 minutes, move it to your dish and mix in rest of salad dressing.
3. Serve the chicken mixture with the tortillas, lettuce, and avocados and let everyone make their own creations.

Nutritional Values: Calories: 783; Fat: 38g; Carbs: 39g; Protein: 72g

18. Orange Chicken and Snap Peas

Prep time: 10 mins | Cook time: 16 mins | Serves: 4

ING:

- two no bones & skin chicken breasts, sliced into 1" pieces
- ½ t. sea salt
- ⅛ t. ground black pepper
- 6 tbs. cornstarch, divided
- 1 c. orange juice
- ¼ c. orange marmalade
- ¼ c. ketchup
- ½ t. ground ginger
- 2 tbs. soy sauce
- 1⅓ c. snap peas

Instructions:

1. Flavor chicken breasts with salt and pepper. Coat it with 4 tablespoons of cornstarch and put on a wire rack to set.
2. In a cake barrel, combine the orange juice, marmalade, ketchup, ginger, soy sauce, and remaining cornstarch. Stir in the snap peas.
3. Warm up your air fryer to 375°Fahrenheit. Put cake barrel in your cooking basket. Cook for 5 mins, stirring once till sauce is thickened. Remove the cake barrel. Put aside.
4. Add chicken to your basket, and cook for ten mins, shaking once.
5. Add chicken to the sauce and snap peas in the cake barrel and stir gently. Return to the basket. Cook for another minute or until the sauce is hot.

Nutritional Values: Calories: 278; Fat: 2g; Carbs: 38g; Protein: 27g

19. Chicken Parm Hoagies

Prep time: 15 mins | Cook time: 8 mins | Serves: 4

ING:

- 2 no bones & skin chicken breasts, sliced into cutlets
- one t. Italian seasoning
- ½ t. sea salt
- one egg
- one egg yolk
- 2 tbs. water
- ½ c. breadcrumbs
- ½ c. Parmesan cheese, grated
- Cooking oil spray
- one c. shredded mozzarella cheese
- 4 hoagie rolls, split & toasted
- 1½ c. marinara sauce, heated

Instructions:

1. Put the chicken cutlets between two sheets of baking paper and pound till about one-fourth". Sprinkle with the Italian seasoning and salt.
2. Put the whole egg plus yolk in your shallow dish and whisk with the water. Put the panko and Parmesan onto a plate and mix.
3. Dip chicken cutlets in your egg mixture, then coat into panko mixture. Put on your rack for 10 minutes.
4. Set the air fryer to 370°F. Put 2 chicken cutlets in your basket and mist using oil.
5. Add a raised rack and add the second 2 cutlets and mist using oil. Cook for 8 mins.
6. Remove your rack, then top all cutlets ¼ cup mozzarella. Let stand until melted.
7. Put the bottoms of the hoagie buns on the work surface. Spread each with 3 tablespoons of marinara sauce.
8. Top with the chicken, 3 tablespoons marinara, then the top half of the buns.

Nutritional Values: Calories: 484; Fat: 17g; Carbs: 38g; Protein: 44g

20. Stir-Fried Chicken with Pineapple

Prep time: 10 mins | Cook time: 11 mins | Serves: 4

ING:

- two no bones & skin chicken breasts, sliced into cubes
- two tbs. cornstarch
- one beaten egg white

- one tbs. olive or peanut oil
- one sliced onion
- one chopped red bell pepper
- 8 ounces cabbed pineapple tidbits, drained, juice reserved
- two tbs. soy sauce

Instructions:

1. Put the chicken breasts into a medium dish. Mix in cornstarch plus egg white. Put aside.
2. In your 6-inch metal dish, mix oil plus onion. Cook in your air fryer for two mins till onion is crisp.
3. Drain chicken, then add to your dish with the onions; stir well. Cook for seven mins.
4. Stir chicken mixture, then add the pepper, pineapple tidbits, 3 tablespoons of the reserved pineapple liquid, plus soy sauce, then mix again.
5. Cook for 2 mins till sauce is slightly thickened.

Nutritional Values: Calories: 291; Fat: 9g; Carbs: 16g; Protein: 35g

21. Chicken Casserole

Prep time: 5 mins | Cook time: 15 mins | Serves: 4

ING:

- twelve ounces cubed no bones & skin chicken breast
- one & ½ pounds Brussels sprouts, halved
- one pound fingerling potatoes, halved
- 2 tbs. paprika
- one tbs. chili powder
- ½ t. red pepper flakes
- One-fourth t. sea salt
- 2 tbs. avocado oil, + more for misting

Instructions:

1. Warm up your air fryer to 400°Fahrenheit.
2. In your big dish, stir together the cubed chicken breast, Brussels sprouts, potatoes, paprika, chili powder, pepper flakes, salt, and avocado oil.
3. Prepare your cooking basket using baking paper. Put chicken mixture, then cook for 10 mins.
4. Stir, mist with more avocado oil, and continue to cook for five mins. Serve.

Nutritional Values: Calories: 378; Fat: 12g; Carbs: 38g; Protein: 35g

22. Chicken Satay

Prep time: 15 mins | Cook time: 6 mins | Serves: 4

ING:

- ½ cup peanut butter, crunchy
- ⅓ cup chicken broth
- three tbs. soy sauce
- two tbs. lemon juice
- two minced cloves garlic
- two tbs. olive oil
- one t. curry powder
- one pound chicken tenders

Instructions:

1. In your med. dish, mix all ingredients except chicken until smooth.
2. Remove 2 tablespoons of this mixture to a small bowl. Put remaining sauce into a serving bowl and set aside.
3. Put chicken tenders to your dish with 2 tablespoons sauce and stir well.
4. Let stand for a few minutes to marinate, then run a bamboo skewer through each chicken tender lengthwise.
5. Put the chicken in your basket and cook within 6 mins. Serve with the reserved sauce.

Nutritional Values: Calories: 448; Fat: 28g; Carbs: 8g; Protein: 46g

23. Balsamic Roasted Chicken Thighs

Prep time: 10 mins | Cook time: 12 mins | Serves: 4

ING:

- ¼ c. balsamic vinegar
- 3 tbs. maple syrup
- 1 t. whole-grain mustard
- 3 minced garlic cloves
- One-half t. each of salt, ground black pepper & smoked paprika
- 1-pound boneless, skinless chicken thighs

Instructions:

1. Warm up your air fryer to 375°Fahrenheit.
2. In your small dish, whisk vinegar, maple syrup, mustard, garlic, salt, pepper, and paprika.

3. Put chicken in your basket, then brush the tops using vinegar mixture, reserving extra.
4. Cook for seven mins, flip chicken, brush the remaining vinegar mixture over the top, and continue cooking for 5 mins. Serve.

Nutritional Values: Calories: 195; Fat: 5g; Carbs: 14g; Protein: 23g

24. Mini Turkey Meatloaves

Prep time: 5 mins | Cook time: 20 mins | Serves: 4

ING:

- ⅓ c. minced onion
- ¼ c. grated carrot
- two garlic cloves, minced
- two tbs. ground almonds
- two t. olive oil
- one t. marjoram, dried
- one egg white
- ¾ lb. ground turkey breast

Instructions:

1. In your med. dish, stir onion, garlic, carrot, almonds, olive oil, marjoram, and egg white.
2. Add the ground turkey. With your hands, gently but -thoroughly mix until combined.
3. Double sixteen foil muffin cup liners and put turkey mixture into each. Bake for twenty mins, then serve immediately.

Nutritional Values: Calories: 141; Fat: 5g; Carbs: 3g; Protein: 23g

25. Tex-Mex Turkey Burgers

Prep time: 10 mins | Cook time: 17 mins | Serves: 4

ING:

- ½ c. salsa, divided
- one large egg, beaten
- three minced cloves garlic
- one jalapeño pepper, minced
- ½ t. sea salt
- ⅛ t. ground black pepper
- one & ¼ pounds ground turkey
- ¼ c. mayonnaise
- four burger buns, split & toasted
- four slices pepper Jack cheese
- four large slices tomato

Instructions:

1. In your big dish, mix ¼ cup of salsa, egg, garlic, jalapeño, salt, plus black pepper. Add the turkey and mix gently. Form into 4 patties.
2. Warm up your air fryer to 375°Fahrenheit. Put patties in your basket, then cook for 17 mins.
3. Meanwhile, in your small dish, combine the mayo plus remaining salsa. Spread some mayo mixture on each half buns.
4. Put cooked turkey burgers, pepper Jack cheese, tomatoes, and more of the mayonnaise mixture, then add the tops of the buns.

Nutritional Values: Calories: 557; Fat: 32g; Carbs: 25g; Protein: 41g

26. Turkey Spinach Meatballs

Prep time: 15 mins | Cook time: 10 mins | Serves: 4

ING:

- two chopped scallions
- one minced garlic clove
- one beaten egg
- one c. frozen cut-leaf spinach, thawed & squeezed dry
- ¼ c. dried breadcrumbs
- ¼ c. grated Parmesan cheese
- one t. dried marjoram
- half t. sea salt
- one-eight t. ground black pepper
- one & ¼ pounds ground turkey

Instructions:

1. In your med. dish, mix scallions, garlic, egg, spinach, breadcrumbs, Parmesan, marjoram, salt, plus pepper.
2. Add the turkey and mix gently but thoroughly. Form into 1½-inch balls.
3. Warm up your air fryer to 400°Fahrenheit. Arrange as many meatballs as can fit in one layer in your basket. Cook the meatballs for ten mins, tossing once.
4. Repeat with the remaining meatballs. Serve.

Nutritional Values: Calories: 295; Fat: 14g; Carbs: 8g; Protein: 34g

27. Cranberry Turkey Quesadillas

Prep time: 10 mins | Cook time: 4 mins | Serves: 4

ING:

- 6 whole-wheat tortillas
- ⅓ c. shredded fat Swiss cheese
- ¾ c. shredded cooked turkey breast
- 2 tbs. cranberry sauce

- 2 tbs. dried cranberries
- ½ t. dried basil
- Olive oil spray

Instructions:

1. Put 3 tortillas on your clean countertop. Evenly put Swiss cheese, turkey, cranberry sauce, and dried cranberries among the tortillas.
2. Sprinkle with the basil and top with the remaining tortillas. Oil outsides of the tortillas using olive oil.
3. One at a time, grill the quesadillas in your air fryer for 4 mins till crisp. Cut into quarters. Serve.

Nutritional Values: Calories: 303; Fat: 6g; Carbs: 41g; Protein: 12g

28. Turkey–Stuffed Zucchini Boats

Prep time: 10 mins | Cook time: 18 mins | Serves: 4

ING:

- two large zucchini, halved lengthwise & scoop the seeds
- 12 ounces ground turkey, 99% lean
- ½ c. red onion, chopped
- one bell pepper, diced
- one c. crushed tomatoes
- two minced garlic cloves
- two tbs. Italian seasoning
- one c. shredded mozzarella cheese

Instructions:

1. Warm up your air fryer to 375°Fahrenheit.
2. In your big dish, stir turkey, onion, bell pepper, crushed tomatoes, garlic, and Italian seasoning. Fill each zucchini boat with one-quarter of the turkey filling.
3. Place each stuffed zucchini boat in your basket, then cook for 15 mins.
4. Once dine, evenly top mozzarella cheese over the zucchini boats, then cook for another 3 minutes. Serve.

Nutritional Values: Calories: 240; Fat: 7g; Carbs: 11g; Protein: 35g

29. Turkey-Stuffed Bell Peppers

Prep time: 10 mins | Cook time: 15 mins | Serves: 4

ING:

- ½ pound lean ground turkey
- 4 medium bell peppers, cut about ½ inch off the tops, cut

- in half lengthwise, & remove seeds
- 15 ounces canned black beans, strained & washed
- one c. Cheddar cheese, shredded
- one c. cooked long-grain brown rice
- one c. mild salsa
- one & one-fourth t. chili powder
- one t. salt
- one-half t. each of ground cumin & black pepper
- oil spray

Instructions:

1. In your big pot over moderately high temp, cook turkey for 5 mins till browned. Drain excess fat.
2. In your big dish, combine the browned turkey, beans, cheese, rice, salsa, chili powder, salt, cumin, and pepper. Spoon the mixture into the bell peppers.
3. Lightly spray your basket using oil. Put stuffed peppers, and air fry within ten mins till warmed throughout. Serve.

Nutritional Values: Calories: 391; Fat: 12g; Carbs: 48g; Protein: 28g

30. Breaded Turkey Cutlets

Prep time: 10 mins | Cook time: 8 mins | Serves: 4

ING:

- ½ c. breadcrumbs
- ¼ t. each of black pepper, paprika, & salt
- ⅛ t. each of garlic powder & dried sage
- one beaten egg
- four turkey breast cutlets

Instructions:

1. Warm up your air fryer to 380°Fahrenheit.
2. In your med. deep dish, mix all dry fixings. Soak each turkey into your egg, then into your dry mixture.
3. Move them in your cooking basket, and bake for four mins, flip them, and bake again within four mins. Serve.

Nutritional Values: Calories: 199; Fat: 4g; Carbs: 10g; Protein: 28g

Chapter 6. BEEF, PORK, AND LAMB RECIPES

31. Steak Bites and Mushrooms

Prep time: 10 mins | Cook time: 10 mins | Serves: 4

ING:

- four tbs. butter
- one onion, chopped
- eight oz button mushrooms, halved
- two minced cloves garlic
- one & ¼ pounds boneless rib-eye or sirloin steak, cut into 1-inch cubes
- ½ t. sea salt
- One-eight t. ground black pepper
- two t. lemon juice
- one t. marjoram, dried
- two tbs. chopped parsley

Instructions:

1. In a cake barrel, combine the butter, onion, mushrooms, garlic, steak cubes, salt, pepper, lemon juice, marjoram, and parsley.
2. Warm up your air fryer to 400°Fahrenheit. Put cake barrel in your basket. Cook for ten mins, stirring once. Serve.

Nutritional Values: Calories: 471; Fat: 38g; Carbs: 6g; Protein: 29g

32. Mongolian Beef

Prep time: 10 mins | Cook time: 13 mins | Serves: 4

ING:

- One lb. flank steak, sliced into ½" -thick strips
- 4 tbs. cornstarch, divided
- ⅛ t. freshly ground black pepper
- Cooking oil spray
- One tbs. grated ginger
- three minced cloves garlic
- ⅔ c. beef stock
- two tbs. soy sauce
- two tbs. brown sugar, light
- two scallions, chopped

Instructions:

1. Put the flank steak in a med. dish and sprinkle with 3 tablespoons of cornstarch and the pepper; toss to coat.

2. Warm up your air fryer to 400°Fahrenheit. Prepare your basket using a round of baking paper that has some holes poked into it.
3. Put the steak in your basket and mist with oil. Cook the beef for 8 mins, shaking once and misting with more oil, until the beef is browned. Remove the beef.
4. In your 7-inch metal dish, combine the remaining cornstarch, the ginger, garlic, stock, soy sauce, brown sugar, and scallions.
5. Put dish in your basket, and cook for five mins, stirring after 3 minutes, until the sauce thickens and is glossy. Toss beef with sauce and serve.

Nutritional Values: Calories: 215; Fat: 6g; Carbs: 14g; Protein: 26g

33. Stir-Fried Steak and Cabbage

Prep time: 15 mins | Cook time: 8 mins | Serves: 4

ING:

- ½ pound sliced into strips sirloin steak
- two t. cornstarch
- one tbs. peanut oil
- two c. chopped red or green cabbage
- one chopped yellow bell pepper
- two chopped green onions
- two cloves garlic, sliced
- ½ c. stir-fry sauce

Instructions:

1. Toss steak with cornstarch. Put aside.
2. In your 6-inch metal dish, combine the peanut oil with the cabbage. Place in your basket, then cook for 3 mins.
3. Remove your dish and put steak, pepper, onions, plus garlic. Cook again for 3 mins.
4. Put stir-fry sauce, then cook for 2 mins till hot. Serve over rice.

Nutritional Values: Calories: 180; Fat: 7g; Carbs: 9g; Protein: 20g

34. Beef Tips and Gravy

Prep time: 10 mins | Cook time: 9 mins | Serves: 4

ING:

- One & one-half pounds cubed sirloin steak
- one tbs. olive oil
- 2 tbs. cornstarch
- 2 cloves garlic, minced
- one t. ground black pepper
- one-half t. salt
- one-half t. smoked paprika

- one-half c. sliced red onion
- one-half c. mushrooms, sliced
- one c. beef broth
- one tbs. unsalted butter

Instructions:

1. Warm up your air fryer to 400°Fahrenheit.
2. In your big dish, mix beef cubes, oil, 1 tablespoon of cornstarch, garlic, pepper, salt, plus paprika.
3. Move it to your 8-inch cooking dish and spread it out in one layer. Cover with the onion and mushrooms.
4. In your small dish, whisk broth and remaining cornstarch.
5. Put cooking dish in your air fryer and cook for 4 mins. Stir and top with the butter and beef broth mixture. Continue cooking for 5 mins. Serve.

Nutritional Values: Calories: 403; Fat: 25g; Carbs: 6g; Protein: 36g

35. Garlic-Herb Rib Eye

Prep time: 10 mins | Cook time: 12 mins | Serves: 2

ING:

- one pound (one" -thick) rib eye steak
- one t. salt
- ½ t. black pepper, ground
- one tbs. butter, unsalted
- one tbs. chopped rosemary
- 2 garlic cloves, minced

Instructions:

1. Warm up your air fryer to 400°Fahrenheit.
2. Flavor steak with salt plus pepper. Put steak in your cooking basket and put butter, rosemary, and garlic.
3. Cook for six mins, flip steak, then continue cooking for six mins. Let sit for 5 minutes. Cut into slices and serve.

Nutritional Values: Calories: 476; Fat: 32g; Carbs: 4g; Protein: 44g

36. Pork Belly Bites

Prep time: 10 mins | Cook time: 12 mins | Serves: 4

ING:

- Oil spray
- one pound pork belly, skinned & cut into 1-inch cubes
- two t. Worcestershire sauce
- one t. soy sauce
- one t. granulated garlic
- ¼ t. salt
- ¼ t. ground black pepper

- ⅓ c. barbecue sauce

Instructions:

1. Prepare your cooking basket using parchment and grease lightly with oil.
2. In your med. dish, combine pork, Worcestershire sauce, soy sauce, garlic, salt, and pepper.
3. Put pork in your basket, and cook at 400°F for 12 mins, flipping twice. Toss with barbecue sauce before serving.

Nutritional Values: Calories: 631; Fat: 60g; Carbs: 10g; Protein: 11g

37. Sweet-and-Sour Polish Sausage

Prep time: 10 mins | Cook time: 10 mins | Serves: 4

ING:

- ¾ pound sliced Polish sausage
- One sliced into strips red bell pepper
- ½ c. minced onion
- 3 tbs. brown sugar
- ⅓ c. ketchup
- two tbs. mustard
- two tbs. apple cider vinegar
- ½ c. chicken broth

Instructions:

1. Put the sausage into a 6-inch metal dish. Add the pepper and minced onion.
2. In your small dish, mix ketchup, sugar, mustard, vinegar, plus broth. Pour into your bowl.
3. Roast it in your air fryer for 10 mins till sauce slightly thickened. Serve.

Nutritional Values: Calories: 381; Fat: 26g; Carbs: 17g; Protein: 19g

38. Honey-Garlic Pork Chops

Prep time: 5 mins | Cook time: 18 mins | Serves: 4

ING:

- Oil, for spraying
- 4 (6-ounce) boneless pork chops
- one t. salt
- half t. black pepper, ground
- ¼ c. honey
- two tbs. minced garlic
- two tbs. lemon juice
- one tbs. sweet chili sauce

Instructions:

1. Prepare your air fryer basket using parchment and grease using oil. Flavor pork chops using salt plus black pepper.
2. Put chops in your basket, then cook at 400°F for 8 mins, flip, and cook for another 7 minutes.
3. In your small pan, mix honey, garlic, lemon juice, plus sweet chili sauce, then simmer on low temp within 3 mins until the sauce thickens.
4. Move chops to your serving plate and pour the sauce on top.

Nutritional Values: Calories: 341; Fat: 12g; Carbs: 20g; Protein: 37g

39. Pork Medallions in Mustard Sauce

Prep time: 10 mins | Cook time: 16 mins | Serves: 4

ING:

- one pound pork tenderloin, sliced into ½-inch-thick rounds
- half t. sea salt
- One-eight t. ground black pepper
- half t. dried marjoram
- 2 tbs. butter
- one tbs. garlic-flavored olive oil
- one small onion, diced
- one c. chicken stock
- two tbs. Dijon mustard
- two tbs. grainy mustard
- ⅓ c. heavy cream

Instructions:

1. Place the pork rounds, cut-side down, between sheets of baking paper, then pound them till about one-fourth" thick. Flavor pork with salt, pepper, plus marjoram.
2. Warm up your air fryer to 350°Fahrenheit. Put pork in your basket, then cook for 5 mins till medallions are almost cooked. Remove pork and wipe out the basket.
3. In a cake barrel, combine the butter, garlic oil, onion, and chicken stock. Set the barrel in your basket and cook for 4 mins.
4. Add two types of mustard and the cream to the barrel. Cook within 4 mins till mixture thickens.
5. Put pork medallions to the sauce in the cake barrel, then cook for 3 mins till hot. Serve.

Nutritional Values: Calories: 259; Fat: 16g; Carbs: 3g; Protein: 25g

40. Lemon Pork Tenderloin

Prep time: 5 mins | Cook time: 10 mins | Serves: 4

ING:

- one (one pound) sliced pork tenderloin
- one tbs. olive oil
- one tbs. lemon juice
- one tbs. honey
- ½ t. lemon zest
- ½ t. marjoram, dried
- salt & ground black pepper, as needed

Instructions:

1. Put pork slices in your med. dish. In your small dish, mix rest of the fixings. Massage the pork slices with marinade.
2. Move them in your air fryer basket and roast for ten mins. Serve.

Nutritional Values: Calories: 209; Fat: 8g; Carbs: 5g; Protein: 30g

41.   Mustard Lamb Chops

Prep time: 5 mins | Cook time: 14 mins | Serves: 4

ING:

- Oil spray
- one tbs. Dijon mustard
- 2 t. lemon juice
- half t. dried tarragon
- one-fourth t. salt
- one-fourth t. black pepper, ground
- 4 (1¼-inch-thick) loin lamb chops

Instructions:

1. Set the air fryer to 390°Fahrenheit. Prepare your cooking basket using parchment and oil spray.
2. In your small dish, mix mustard, lemon juice, tarragon, salt, plus black pepper.
3. Pat dry lamb chops with a paper towel. Brush the chops with mustard mixture.
4. Put lamb chops in your basket, and cook for eight mins, flip, and cook for another six mins. Serve.

Nutritional Values: Calories: 341; Fat: 29g; Carbs: 1g; Protein: 18g

42.   Savory Lamb Chops

Prep time: 10 mins | Cook time: 18 mins | Serves: 4

ING:

- ½ cup chicken broth
- two tbs. red currant or raspberry jelly
- two tbs. Dijon mustard
- one tbs. fresh lemon juice
- half t. dried thyme
- 8 lamb loin chops (4 to 5 ounces each)
- half t. sea salt
- one-eight t. black pepper, ground

Instructions:

1. In your small dish, combine chicken broth, jelly, mustard, lemon juice, and thyme.
2. Flavor chops with salt plus pepper, then brush with some broth mixture.
3. Warm up your air fryer to 375°Fahrenheit. Put 4 chops in one layer in your cooking basket. Add a raised rack and top with the remaining chops.
4. Cook the chops for fifteen mins. Put all chops and the remaining chicken broth mixture in a cake barrel.
5. Put in your basket and cook for 3 mins till sauce is simmering. Serve.

Nutritional Values: Calories: 356; Fat: 16g; Carbs: 8g; Protein: 45g

43. Herbed Lamb Steaks

Prep time: 10 mins | Cook time: 15 mins | Serves: 4

ING:

- ½ medium onion
- two tbs. minced garlic
- two t. ground ginger
- one t. each of ground cinnamon, onion powder, cayenne pepper & salt
- 4 (6-ounce) boneless lamb sirloin steaks
- Oil spray

Instructions:

1. In your blender, mix onion, garlic, ginger, cinnamon, onion powder, cayenne pepper, plus salt. Pulse until minced.
2. Place the lamb steaks in your big dish and sprinkle onion mixture over. Turn the steaks until they are evenly coated. Cover and chill for 30 mins.
3. Warm up your air fryer to 330°Fahrenheit. Prepare your cooking basket using parchment and oil spray.
4. Put lamb steaks in one layer in your basket, cook for 8 mins, flip, then cook for 7 mins. Serve.

Nutritional Values: Calories: 368; Fat: 24g; Carbs: 3g; Protein: 32g

44. Air Fryer Lamb Meatballs

Prep time: 10 mins | Cook time: 12 mins | Serves: 4

ING:

- one pound ground lamb
- 1 t. cumin ground
- 2 t. powdered onion
- 2 tbs. minced parsley
- ¼ t. cinnamon ground
- Salt & pepper, as required

Instructions:

1. Mix all the ingredients in a dish and form it into meatballs. Move them in your cooking basket.
2. Cook for 12 minutes at 350 Fahrenheit, tossing once. Serve.

Nutritional Values: Calories: 328; Fat: 22g; Carbs: 1g; Protein: 28g

45. Rosemary Lamb Chops

Prep time: 5 mins | Cook time: 15 mins | Serves: 4

ING:

- 8 (3-ounce) lamb chops
- two t. olive oil
- one & ½ t. rosemary, chopped
- one minced garlic clove
- Salt & pepper, as needed

Instructions:

1. Drizzle the lamb chops using oil.
2. In your small dish, combine rosemary, garlic, salt plus pepper. Rub it on each lamb chop.
3. Place the lamb chops in your air fryer basket and cook for 10 mins. Flip lamb chops and cook for an additional 5 mins. Cool before serving.

Nutritional Values: Calories: 308; Fat: 17g; Carbs: 1g; Protein: 35g

Chapter 7. FISH AND SEAFOOD RECIPES

46. California Fish Tacos

Prep time: 10 mins | Cook time: 8 mins | Serves: 4

ING:

- one lemon, thinly sliced
- 16 ounces red snapper or halibut fish fillets
- one tbs. olive oil
- one tbs. chili powder
- ½ t. salt
- 2 c. shredded coleslaw mix with carrots
- 2 tbs. orange juice
- ½ cup salsa
- 4 (10-inch) flour tortillas
- ½ cup sour cream
- 2 avocados, sliced

Instructions:

1. Arrange the lemon slices in the bottom of your basket.
2. Warm up your air fryer to 350°Fahrenheit. Drizzle fish fillets using oil, then flavor with chili powder plus salt.
3. Put fillets on your basket. Cook for 6 mins till fish flakes.
4. Meanwhile, in your big dish, toss coleslaw mix, orange juice, plus salsa.
5. Once the fish is done, remove it from the air fryer basket and cover. Discard lemons.
6. Wrap the tortillas in foil and put them in your basket. Cook for two mins till heated.
7. Put fish in the tortillas, then top with cabbage mixture, sour cream, add avocados. Serve.

Nutritional Values: Calories: 539; Fat: 29g; Carbs: 44g; Protein: 30g

47. Cilantro Butter Baked Mahi Mahi

Prep time: 5 mins | Cook time: 12 mins | Serves: 4

ING:

- two tbs. butter, melted
- two tbs. chopped cilantro
- two minced garlic cloves
- half t. salt
- one-fourth t. black pepper, ground
- one-fourth t. chili powder
- 4 (4-ounce) boneless, skinless mahi mahi fillets

Instructions:
1. Warm up your air fryer to 375°Fahrenheit.
2. In your small dish, mix butter, cilantro, garlic, salt, pepper, plus chili powder. Spread the butter mixture on each fillet.
3. Place a piece of parchment paper in your cooking basket. Put fish and cook for 6 mins.
4. Flip and cook again for 6 mins till flaky. Serve immediately.

Nutritional Values: Calories: 157; Fat: 7g; Carbs: 1g; Protein: 21g

48. Honey-Balsamic Salmon

Prep time: 5 mins | Cook time: 7 mins | Serves: 2

ING:

- Oil spray
- two (6-ounce) salmon fillets
- ¼ c. balsamic vinegar
- two tbs. honey
- two t. red pepper flakes
- two t. olive oil
- half t. salt
- one-fourth t. black pepper, ground

Instructions:

1. Prepare your cooking basket using parchment and oil spray. Put salmon inside.
2. In your small dish, mix vinegar, oil, honey, salt, pepper flakes, add black pepper. Brush the mixture over the salmon.
3. Cook at 390°Fahrenheit for 7 mins. Serve immediately.

Nutritional Values: Calories: 373; Fat: 15g; Carbs: 23g; Protein: 34g

49. Sriracha Tuna Melt

Prep time: 10 mins | Cook time: 7 mins | Serves: 4

ING:

- two English muffins
- two tbs. butter
- one (twelve ounces) can light tuna, strained
- ⅓ c. mayonnaise
- two tbs. Dijon mustard
- one tbs. lemon juice
- ⅓ c. chopped celery
- ½ t. sriracha sauce
- 4 slices tomato
- 4 slices Swiss cheese

Instructions:

1. Split the English muffins with a fork. Spread each of the 4 halves with butter.
2. Warm up your air fryer to 375°Fahrenheit. Put muffin halves in your basket and cook for 3 mins till toasted. Remove from the air fryer and put aside.
3. In your med. dish, mix tuna, mayo, mustard, lemon juice, celery, add sriracha. Put it among English muffin halves.
4. Top each of the sandwiches with a tomato slice and a cheese slice. Place then cook for 4 mins. Serve.

Nutritional Values: Calories: 425; Fat: 29g; Carbs: 16g; Protein: 26g

50. Baked Chili-Lime Tilapia

Prep time: 5 mins | Cook time: 8 mins | Serves: 4

ING:

- half t. salt
- half t. black pepper, ground
- one-fourth t. each of garlic powder, chili powder & smoked paprika
- 4 (4-ounce) tilapia fillets
- 2 tbs. lime juice

Instructions:

1. Warm up your air fryer to 400°Fahrenheit. Prepare your basket using baking paper.
2. In your small dish, mix all the seasonings. Place the fish fillets in your shallow dish.
3. Pour lime juice over fillets, then flavor with seasoning blend, making sure to coat all sides well. Put fish in your basket, then cook for 4 mins.
4. Flip and cook within four mins till crispy. Serve immediately.

Nutritional Values: Calories: 112; Fat: 2g; Carbs: 1g; Protein: 23g

51. Garlic-Dill Salmon with Tomatoes

Prep time: 5 mins | Cook time: 12 mins | Serves: 4

ING:

- four tbs. butter, unsalted
- four minced garlic cloves
- ¼ c. chopped dill
- ½ t. salt
- ½ t. black pepper, ground
- four (four -ounce) wild-caught salmon fillets, skin removed
- one lemon, thinly sliced

- one-pound green beans, trimmed
- one c. halved cherry tomatoes

Instructions:

1. Warm up your air fryer to 390°Fahrenheit. Prepare your basket using baking paper.
2. In your small dish, mix butter, garlic, dill, salt, and pepper. Brush butter mixture over the fillets.
3. Place salmon in the basket in one layer. Place about three-quarters of the lemon slices on top.
4. Place green beans and tomatoes around fillets. Cook for 12 mins. Serve with the remaining lemon slices.

Nutritional Values: Calories: 312; Fat: 19g; Carbs: 11g; Protein: 25g

52. Lemon-Herb Tuna Steaks

Prep time: 20 mins | Cook time: 7 mins | Serves: 4

ING:

- ½ tbs. olive oil
- one minced garlic clove
- one-fourth t. salt
- one-fourth t. chili powder
- one tbs. + one t. lemon juice
- one tbs. chopped fresh cilantro
- four (four ounces) tuna steaks
- one lemon, thinly sliced

Instructions:

1. In your wide, shallow dish, mix oil, garlic, salt, chili powder, lemon juice, plus cilantro.
2. Mix in tuna steaks, cover loosely, and set aside to marinate for 20 minutes.
3. Warm up your air fryer to 380°Fahrenheit. Place parchment paper in your basket.
4. Put marinated tuna steaks in your basket in one layer. Discard any remaining marinade.
5. Cook for 7 minutes. Remove basket and let stand for five mins. Top with lemon slices, then serve.

Nutritional Values: Calories: 143; Fat: 2g; Carbs: 1g; Protein: 28g

53. Parmesan Garlic Shrimp

Prep time: 5 mins | Cook time: 8 mins | Serves: 4

ING:

- One & ¼ pounds large shrimp, peel it & devein it
- One tbs. olive oil
- One tbs. lemon juice
- ½ t. garlic powder
- 2 garlic cloves, minced
- ½ c. grated Parmesan cheese

Instructions:

1. Put the shrimp in a big dish and sprinkle with oil, lemon juice, add garlic powder. Mix in minced garlic plus Parmesan.
2. Warm up your air fryer to 350°Fahrenheit. Place shrimp in your basket. Cook shrimp for 8 mins, tossing once. Serve.

Nutritional Values: Calories: 187; Fat: 8g; Carbs: 4g; Protein: 23g

54. Lemony Sea Scallops

Prep time: 5 mins | Cook time: 8 mins | Serves: 4

ING:

- 16 to 24 sea scallops, patted-dry
- ½ t. sea salt
- One-eight t. black pepper, ground
- two tbs. butter, melted
- One t. lemon zest
- two tbs. lemon juice

Instructions:

1. Flavor scallops with the salt plus pepper, then place in your med. dish.
2. In your small dish, mix melted butter, zest, plus lemon juice. Drizzle half of this mixture over the scallops.
3. Warm up your air fryer to 400°Fahrenheit. Put the scallops in your basket. Cook for 8 mins, turning scallops once, until they are opaque.
4. Remove and top with the remaining lemon mixture. Serve.

Nutritional Values: Calories: 149; Fat: 7g; Carbs: 1g; Protein: 21g

55. Crispy Calamari

Prep time: 10 mins | Cook time: 8 mins | Serves: 4

ING:

- Oil spray
- ¼ c. flour, all-purpose
- two t. salt, + more if desired
- two t. black pepper, ground
- one big egg
- one-pound calamari rings

Instructions:

1. Warm up your air fryer to 350°Fahrenheit. Prepare your basket using parchment and oil spray.
2. Combine flour, salt, plus black pepper in your zip-top plastic bag and set aside.
3. In your medium dish, whisk egg, put calamari, and mix well. Transfer calamari to your zip-top bag, seal, then shake well until evenly coated.
4. Put calamari in your basket and grease lightly using oil. Cook for five mins, flip, spray with oil, then cook again within three mins, until crispy and cooked through.
5. Sprinkle with additional salt, if desired, and serve.

Nutritional Values: Calories: 161; Fat: 4g; Carbs: 10g; Protein: 20g

56. Shrimp and Crab Cakes

Prep time: 10 mins | Cook time: 10 mins | Serves: 4

ING:

- one cup lump crabmeat
- one cup chopped cooked shrimp
- three chopped scallions
- one beaten egg
- ¼ cup mayonnaise
- 2 tablespoons honey mustard
- ¾ cup saltine cracker crumbs, divided
- one tablespoon fresh lemon juice
- Cooking oil spray

Instructions:

1. In your med. dish, mix crabmeat, shrimp, scallions, egg, mayo, honey mustard, ¼ cup of cracker crumbs, and the lemon juice.
2. Form into 4 patties. Sprinkle with the remaining ½ cup of cracker crumbs on both sides. Mist with cooking spray.

3. Warm up your air fryer to 375°Fahrenheit. Prepare your basket using a round of baking paper that has holes punched into it.
4. Coat the paper with cooking spray. Put the patties on the parchment paper. Cook for ten mins till golden. Serve.

Nutritional Values: Calories: 230; Fat: 14g; Carbs: 14g; Protein: 13g

Chapter 8. SIDE DISHES

57. Roasted Spicy Corn

Prep time: 5 mins | Cook time: 15 mins | Serves: 4

ING:

- two c. frozen corn kernels, thawed & drained
- one onion, diced
- two garlic cloves, sliced
- two tbs. butter, melted
- one t. chili powder
- half t. cayenne pepper
- half t. sea salt
- one-eight t. ground black pepper
- one-fourth c. double/single cream

Instructions:

1. Combine the corn, onion, garlic, butter, chili powder, cayenne, salt, add black pepper in your 6-inch metal dish that fits into your basket.
2. Warm up your air fryer to 400°Fahrenheit. Put bowl in your basket and roast for 10 mins, shaking the basket once, until some of the kernels start to turn gold.
3. Remove the basket and pour the cream over the corn; stir to mix. Roast again for 5 mins till cream has thickened slightly. Serve.

Nutritional Values: Calories: 180; Fat: 12g; Carbs: 18g; Protein: 3g

58. Crispy Mushrooms

Prep time: 10 mins | Cook time: 6 mins | Serves: 4

ING:

- one (8-ounce) package cremini mushrooms, cut into quarters
- ⅓ c. flour, all-purpose
- one egg, beaten
- two-third c. panko breadcrumbs
- half t. smoked paprika
- half t. salt
- one-eight t. ground black pepper
- Cooking oil, for misting

Instructions:

1. Put flour on your plate and the egg in your deep dish. On a separate plate, combine the panko, smoked paprika, salt, add pepper.
2. Dip mushrooms in your flour, then egg, and in your panko mixture.

3. Place coated mushrooms on a wire rack as you work. Warm up your air fryer to 400°Fahrenheit. Add mushrooms to your basket.
4. Mist lightly with oil. Cook mushrooms for 6 minutes, flipping them over halfway through, until they are crisp.
5. Repeat with remaining mushrooms. Serve.

Nutritional Values: Calories: 94; Fat: 2g; Carbs: 15g; Protein: 5g

59. Roasted Carrots

Prep time: 5 mins | Cook time: 18 mins | Serves: 4

ING:

- two c. baby carrots, patted dry
- one big carrot, peeled & sliced ½ inch thick
- one tbs. orange juice
- two t. olive oil
- one t. butter, dissolved
- one t. dill weed, dried
- half t. sea salt
- One-eight t. black pepper, ground

Instructions:

1. Put carrots in your air fryer basket.
2. In your small dish, mix orange juice, oil, butter, dill weed, salt, add pepper. Pour over carrots and toss to coat.
3. Warm up your air fryer to 400°Fahrenheit. Roast for 10 mins, shake and roast for another 8 mins till tender and glazed. Serve.

Nutritional Values: Calories: 61; Fat: 3g; Carbs: 8g; Protein: 1g

60. Parmesan Asparagus

Prep time: 5 mins | Cook time: 7 mins | Serves: 4

ING:

- one-pound fresh asparagus, trimmed
- one tbs. olive oil
- one t. lemon juice
- half t. sea salt
- One-eight t. black pepper, ground
- three tbs. grated Parmesan cheese

Instructions:

1. Put asparagus in your cooking basket, then mix in oil, lemon juice, salt plus pepper. Toss with Parmesan cheese.

2. Warm up your air fryer to 400°Fahrenheit. Roast for 7 mins, shaking once. Serve.

Nutritional Values: Calories: 87; Fat: 7g; Carbs: 5g; Protein: 6g

61. Five-Spice Broccoli

Prep time: 5 mins | Cook time: 13 mins | Serves: 4

ING:

- one bunch broccoli, florets
- 2 tbs. olive oil
- one t. five-spice powder
- one-fourth t. onion powder
- one-fourth t. sea salt
- ⅛ t. ground black pepper

Instructions:

1. Put broccoli into your big dish, then coat with oil. Sprinkle with the five-spice powder, onion powder, salt, add pepper. Mix well. Put the broccoli into your basket.
2. Warm up your air fryer to 400°Fahrenheit. Roast the broccoli for 8 mins. Shake basket and roast for another 5 mins. Serve immediately.

Nutritional Values: Calories: 99; Fat: 7g; Carbs: 8g; Protein: 3g

62. Caramelized Sweet Potatoes

Prep time: 5 mins | Cook time: 18 mins | Serves: 4

ING:

- two sweet potatoes, peeled & cubed
- two tbs. maple syrup
- one tbs. butter, melted
- one tbs. brown sugar
- ½ t. sea salt
- Pinch nutmeg

Instructions:

1. Put sweet potatoes in your cooking basket.
2. In your small dish, combine maple syrup, butter, sugar, salt, add nutmeg. Drizzle half of this mixture over the sweet potatoes, tossing to coat.
3. Warm up your air fryer to 400°Fahrenheit. Roast the potatoes for 10 mins. Toss the potatoes, put rest of the butter mixture, and toss again.
4. Continue cooking for another 8 mins. Serve.

Nutritional Values: Calories: 116; Fat: 3g; Carbs: 22g; Protein: 1g

63. Roasted Italian Bell Peppers

Prep time: 10 mins | Cook time: 8 mins | Serves: 4

ING:

- one each of red, yellow, & orange bell pepper, sliced
- one tbs. olive oil
- one t. lemon juice
- one t. dried Italian seasoning
- ½ t. sea salt
- ⅛ t. black pepper, ground
- ¼ c. chopped fresh flat-leaf parsley

Instructions:

1. Combine all bell peppers in your basket. Toss in oil, lemon juice, Italian seasoning, salt, plus pepper.
2. Warm up your air fryer to 350°Fahrenheit. Roast for 8 mins, shaking once till tender. Top with parsley and serve.

Nutritional Values: Calories: 69; Fat: 3g; Carbs: 8g; Protein: 2g

Chapter 9. VEGAN RECIPES

64. Chili-Lime Bean and Rice Burritos

Prep time: 10 mins | Cook time: 10 mins | Serves: 4

ING:

- one thinly sliced bell pepper
- ½ thinly sliced red onion
- ½ c. sliced mushrooms
- two garlic cloves, peeled
- one tbs. olive oil
- one c. brown rice, cooked
- one (fifteen-ounce) can pinto beans, strained & washed
- ½ t. salt
- One-fourth t. each of chili powder, ground cumin & smoked paprika
- one tbs. lime juice
- 4 whole-wheat tortillas

Instructions:

1. Warm up your air fryer to 400°Fahrenheit.
2. In your med. dish, toss bell pepper, onion, mushrooms, garlic, add olive oil.
3. Transfer the mixture to your basket and cook for 5 mins. Stir and cook for 5 mins. Remove garlic mixture, then mince.
4. In your big dish, mix the brown rice, pinto beans, salt, chili powder, cumin, paprika, minced garlic, and lime juice.
5. Put one-fourth roasted vegetable mixture in your whole-wheat tortillas. Top with a quarter of the rice mixture.
6. Fold and carefully roll up to secure filling. Repeat with the remaining tortillas and filling. Serve immediately.

Nutritional Values: Calories: 328; Fat: 8g; Carbs: 53g; Protein: 12g

65. Roasted Garlic Brussels Sprouts

Prep time: 10 mins | Cook time: 17 mins | Serves: 4

ING:

- one pound Brussels sprouts, halved
- one tbs. olive oil
- one tbs. lemon juice
- ½ t. sea salt
- ⅛ t. garlic powder
- 4 garlic cloves, thinly sliced

Instructions:

1. In your medium dish, mix oil, lemon juice, salt, add garlic powder. Toss in halved Brussels sprouts.
2. Warm up your air fryer to 375°Fahrenheit. Put Brussels sprouts in your basket. Cook for 15 mins, shaking basket once, until the sprouts are light golden brown.
3. Toss the sprouts with garlic. Cook for two mins more till garlic is light golden brown.

Nutritional Values: Calories: 84; Fat: 4g; Carbs: 11g; Protein: 4g

66. Garlicky Green Beans

Prep time: 5 mins | Cook time: 9 mins | Serves: 4

ING:

- One & ½ pounds green beans, trimmed
- One tbs. olive oil
- half t. garlic powder
- half t. sea salt
- one-eight t. ground black pepper
- 4 garlic cloves, thinly sliced

Instructions:

1. In your dish, mix beans, oil, garlic powder, sea salt, add pepper.
2. Warm up your air fryer to 375°Fahrenheit. Add green beans to your basket. Cook for 6 mins, shaking the basket once.
3. Add the garlic, shake, and cook for another 3 mins till green beans are tender.

Nutritional Values: Calories: 88; Fat: 4g; Carbs: 13g; Protein: 3g

67. Steamed Green Veggie Trio

Prep time: 5 mins | Cook time: 9 mins | Serves: 4

ING:

- two c. broccoli florets
- one c. green beans
- one tbs. olive oil
- one tbs. lemon juice
- one c. frozen baby peas
- two tbs. honey mustard
- Pinch salt & ground black pepper

Instructions:

1. Put the broccoli and green beans in your basket. Put 2 tablespoons water in your air fryer pan.

2. Toss vegetables with oil and lemon juice. Steam for 6 mins, remove basket and add peas. Steam for 3 mins.
3. Move the vegetables to your serving dish, drizzle with honey mustard, salt and pepper. Toss well and serve.

Nutritional Values: Calories: 99; Fat: 4g; Carbs: 13g; Protein: 4g

68. Roasted Waldorf Salad

Prep time: 10 mins | Cook time: 12 mins | Serves: 4

ING:

- two apples, seeded & sliced
- two t. olive oil, divided
- 1½ c. red grapes
- ½ c. vegan mayonnaise
- two tbs. lemon juice
- one tbs. agave syrup
- 3 celery stalks, sliced
- ½ c. coarsely chopped pecans

Instructions:

1. Put the chopped apples in your basket and coat with 1 teaspoon oil.
2. Warm up your air fryer for 400°Fahrenheit. Roast for 4 mins, remove basket, put grapes and remaining olive oil. Toss again.
3. Roast again for 8 mins, shaking basket once, until tender.
4. Meanwhile, whisk mayo, lemon juice, plus agave syrup in your med. dish. Mix in celery plus pecans.
5. Put roasted apples plus grapes in your salad dressing dish and stir gently. Serve or refrigerate for 2 hours before serving.

Nutritional Values: Calories: 408; Fat: 33g; Carbs: 29g; Protein: 2g

69. Stir-Fried Zucchini and Yellow Squash

Prep time: 15 mins | Cook time: 9 mins | Serves: 4

ING:

- one medium zucchini, sliced into ½-inch rounds
- two medium yellow squash, sliced into ½-inch rounds
- 3 cloves garlic, sliced
- two tbs. olive oil
- ⅓ c. veg. broth
- one tbs. lemon juice
- two t. cornstarch
- one t. dried basil
- ½ t. sea salt
- ⅛ t. black pepper, ground

Instructions:

1. In your 7-inch metal dish, combine the squash, zucchini, garlic, and olive oil.
2. Warm up your air fryer to 400°Fahrenheit. Put dish in your basket, then cook the zucchini mixture for 5 mins, stirring once. Drain if necessary.
3. Meanwhile, in your small dish, mix broth, lemon juice, cornstarch, basil, salt, and pepper.
4. Stir in broth mixture into your zucchini. Cook for another 4 mins, stirring twice. Serve.

Nutritional Values: Calories: 93; Fat: 7g; Carbs: 7g; Protein: 2g

70. Crispy Fried Okra

Prep time: 5 mins | Cook time: 10 mins | Serves: 4

ING:

- 2 cups okra, cut into ½-inch rounds
- one tbs. olive oil
- one garlic clove, minced
- half t. salt
- half t. black pepper, ground

Instructions:

1. In your medium dish, mix all fixings till okra is evenly coated.
2. Transfer it to your basket and cook for five mins at 350°Fahrenheit. Shake basket and cook for five mins. Serve immediately.

Nutritional Values: Calories: 47; Fat: 3g; Carbs: 4g; Protein: 1g

71. Herbed Vegetable Mélange

Prep time: 10 mins | Cook time: 14 mins | Serves: 4

ING:

- one sliced red bell pepper
- Eight ounces of package mushrooms, sliced
- one sliced yellow summer squash
- three sliced cloves garlic
- one tbs. olive oil
- ½ t. dried thyme
- ½ t. dried basil
- ½ t. dried tarragon

Instructions:

1. Place the pepper, mushrooms, squash, garlic, add oil in a medium dish. Toss well, put thyme, basil, plus tarragon. Mix well.
2. Move them in your basket. Roast for 14 mins till vegetables are tender.

Nutritional Values: Calories: 63; Fat: 4g; Carbs: 6g; Protein: 3g

72. Crispy Ginger Edamame

Prep time: 5 mins | Cook time: 10 mins | Serves: 4

ING:

- two cups shelled frozen edamame, thawed
- two tbs. coconut aminos
- two t. grated ginger
- two tbs. sesame seeds
- two tbs. hemp seeds
- two tbs. olive oil

Instructions:

1. Warm up your air fryer to 375°Fahrenheit. Put edamame in your medium dish.
2. In your small dish, whisk aminos, ginger, sesame seeds, hemp seeds, and oil.
3. Toss half amino mixture with edamame and move it in your basket. Cook for 8 mins, shaking once.
4. Once done, transfer the edamame to a medium dish, toss with rest of coconut aminos mixture. Serve.

Nutritional Values: Calories: 243; Fat: 16g; Carbs: 12g; Protein: 11g

73. Roasted Cherry Tomatoes

Prep time: 10 mins | Cook time: 8 mins | Serves: 4

ING:

- one tbs. dried oregano
- one tbs. dried basil
- two t. dried marjoram
- one t. dried thyme
- one t. salt
- two c. cherry tomatoes, stemmed
- one tbs. olive oil

Instructions:

1. In your small dish, mix oregano, basil, marjoram, thyme, add salt. Transfer to your small screw-top glass jar.
2. Set the air fryer to 400°F. Prick each cherry tomato with a toothpick to prevent bursting.
3. Put the tomatoes and olive oil on your heavy-duty aluminum foil. Toss with 1½ teaspoons of the herb mix and toss.

4. Fold the foil around the tomatoes, leaving air space in the packet, and seal loosely.
5. Put the foil packet in your air fryer. Cook for 8 mins until tomatoes are tender.

Nutritional Values: Calories: 46; Fat: 4g; Carbs: 4g; Protein: 1g

Chapter 10. APPETIZERS RECIPES

74. Jalapeño Poppers

Prep time: 10 mins | Cook time: 10 mins | Serves: 6

ING:

- 12 jalapeño peppers, stemmed, halved & seeded
- 4 ounces cream cheese
- 2 tbs. mayonnaise
- one c. Cheddar cheese, shredded
- one-fourth c. Parmesan cheese, grated
- flour, for dusting
- one sheet puff pastry, frozen & thawed

Instructions:

1. In your medium dish, mix cream cheese plus mayo until smooth. Mix in Cheddar and Parmesan cheeses.
2. Fill 12 of the jalapeño pepper halves with equal parts of this mixture, then top them with the other pepper half to make 12 poppers.
3. Dust your work surface using flour. Roll out your puff pastry into a 12" square.
4. Cut them in half, then cut each half into twelve 1-by-6-inch rectangular strips.
5. Wind a puff pastry strip around a filled jalapeño half in a spiral shape. Repeat for all the puff pastry strips and stuffed jalapeños.
6. Put the filled and wrapped jalapeño peppers in your basket.
7. Warm up your air fryer to 400°Fahrenheit. Air-fry for 10 mins or until pastry is golden brown. Serve.

Nutritional Values: Calories: 238; Fat: 20g; Carbs: 6g; Protein: 9g

75. Spinach-Cranberry Turnovers

Prep time: 10 mins | Cook time: 11 mins | Serves: 6

ING:

- four ounces cream cheese
- two tbs. sour cream
- one c. chopped spinach
- one-third c. dried cranberries, chopped
- three (9-x-14") sheets phyllo dough, frozen & thawed
- three tbs. melted butter

Instructions:

1. In your medium dish, beat cream cheese plus sour cream. Stir in spinach plus cranberries until well mixed. Put aside.
2. Place phyllo dough on your work surface, then cover using damp towel. Remove one sheet of phyllo and cut it into four 3½-by-9-inch rectangles.
3. Put tbsp of filling on each rectangle, with the short side facing you.
4. Fold the phyllo into triangles, then brush using butter to seal. Do same with rest of phyllo, filling, and butter.
5. Set the air fryer to 375°F. Put 4 to 6 triangles in your basket. Bake for 11 mins, turning once. Repeat with the remaining turnovers. Serve.

Nutritional Values: Calories: 189; Fat: 14g; Carbs: 15g; Protein: 3g

76. Apricots in Blankets

Prep time: 15 mins | Cook time: 8 mins | Serves: 6

ING:

- 6 dried apricots, halved lengthwise
- 4 tbs. cream cheese
- ½ sheet frozen puff pastry, thawed
- 4 tbs. honey mustard
- 2 tbs. butter, melted

Instructions:

1. Stuff each apricot with teaspoon of cream cheese. Put aside.
2. Roll out puff pastry until it is 6 by 12 inches. Cut in 1/2 lengthwise for 2 (3-x-12") rectangles.
3. Slice each rectangle into six 3-inch strips for a total of 12 puff pastry strips.
4. Spread 1 teaspoon of honey mustard onto each strip. Place a filled apricot on each strip and roll up the pastry, pinching the seam closed but leaving the ends open.
5. Place 6 filled pastries in your basket. Brush each with some melted butter.
6. Warm up your air fryer to 375°Fahrenheit. Bake for 8 mins till pastry is golden brown. Repeat with the other six pastries, then serve.

Nutritional Values: Calories: 137; Fat: 9g; Carbs: 12g; Protein: 2g

77. Tex-Mex Cheese Sticks

Prep time: 10 mins | Cook time: 7 mins | Serves: 4

ING:

- one egg, beaten
- ½ c. dried breadcrumbs
- ¼ c. ground peanuts
- 1 tbs. chili powder
- ¼ t. red pepper flakes
- ⅛ t. cayenne pepper
- 8 mozzarella string cheese sticks
- Cooking oil, for misting

Instructions:

1. Place the beaten egg in your shallow dish. Combine breadcrumbs, peanuts, chili powder, pepper flakes, add cayenne on a plate.
2. Soak each string cheese in the egg then in your bread crumb mixture.
3. Put the sticks on your cooking tray lined with baking paper and freeze for thirty mins.
4. Repeat the breading routine. Freeze sticks for another 30 minutes.
5. Warm up your air fryer to 375°Fahrenheit. Place 4 sticks in your basket in a one layer, then grease them using oil.
6. Cook for 7 mins till golden. Repeat with the remaining sticks. Serve hot.

Nutritional Values: Calories: 299; Fat: 19g; Carbs: 14g; Protein: 19g

78. Buffalo Cauliflower Bites

Prep time: 10 mins | Cook time: 12 mins | Serves: 6

ING:

- one big cauliflower head, broken into florets
- 3 tbs. hot sauce
- two tbs. butter, dissolved
- one tbs. honey
- ½ c. dried breadcrumbs
- oil spray

Instructions:

1. In a big dish, mix cauliflower, hot sauce, butter, plus honey. Toss the cauliflower with the breadcrumbs.
2. Put florets in one layer in your basket. Spritz using oil spray.
3. Warm up your air fryer to 375°Fahrenheit and roast for twelve mins, shaking once, until the cauliflower is crisp. Serve warm with more hot sauce.

Nutritional Values: Calories: 116; Fat: 5g; Carbs: 17g; Protein: 4g

79. Tandoori-Style Chickpeas

Prep time: 5 mins | Cook time: 10 mins | Serves: 6

ING:

- Fifteen ounces canned chickpeas, strained & washed, patted dry
- oil spray
- two t. curry powder
- one t. smoked paprika
- one t. ground cumin
- ½ t. cayenne pepper

Instructions:

1. Put chickpeas in your cooking basket.
2. Warm up your air fryer to 400°Fahrenheit. Roast the chickpeas for 5 mins.
3. Spritz chickpeas using oil spray, then toss well. Roast for 8 mins more, shaking the basket once.
4. Meanwhile, in your small dish, mix curry powder, paprika, cumin, and cayenne pepper.
5. Remove your cooking basket and toss in spice mixture. Continue roasting for 2 minutes or until the chickpeas are fragrant.
6. Let the chickpeas cool for about 10 minutes, then serve.

Nutritional Values: Calories: 72; Fat: 1g; Carbs: 12g; Protein: 4g

80. Roasted Garlic and Onion Dip

Prep time: 10 mins | Cook time: 20 mins | Serves: 6

ING:

- 2 heads garlic, cut the top
- 1 tbs. olive oil
- Eight ounces package cream cheese
- ½ c. mayonnaise
- two tbs. heavy cream
- ¼ t. sea salt
- 3 scallions, sliced
- 1 tbs. minced fresh chives

Instructions:

1. Drizzle each garlic head with the olive oil. Loosely wrap garlic heads in your foil and place in your basket.
2. Warm up your air fryer to 400°Fahrenheit. Roast the garlic for 20 mins, until the garlic cloves are soft.

3. Remove the foil packets, unwrap the garlic heads, and cool on your wire rack for 20 mins.
4. Separate garlic cloves and remove the papery skins; place the cloves in your med. dish. Mash until smooth.
5. Beat cream cheese, mayo, heavy cream, and salt until smooth.
6. Beat in the roasted garlic paste until well mixed, then mix in scallions and chives. Serve.

Nutritional Values: Calories: 299; Fat: 31g; Carbs: 3g; Protein: 3g

Chapter 11. SNACK RECIPES

81. Cajun-Spiced Roasted Pecans

Prep time: 5 mins | Cook time: 6 mins | Serves: 4

ING:

- One-fourth t. each of black pepper ground, chili powder & salt
- One-eight t. each of cayenne pepper, dried thyme, garlic powder & onion powder
- 1 cup raw pecans
- 2 tbs. butter, melted

Instructions:

1. Warm up your air fryer to 300°Fahrenheit.
2. In your small dish, whisk black pepper, chili powder, salt, cayenne, thyme, garlic, and onion powder. Put aside.
3. In your medium dish, toss pecans plus butter. Toss in spice mixture.
4. Transfer the pecans to your basket and cook for 3 mins. Shake the pecans and cook for another 3 mins. Serve.

Nutritional Values: Calories: 224; Fat: 24g; Carbs: 4g; Protein: 2g

82. Crispy Sweet Potato Fries

Prep time: 10 mins | Cook time: 12 mins | Serves: 4

ING:

- two big, sweet potatoes, peeled & sliced
- 1 tbs. olive oil
- 1 t. salt
- half t. black pepper, ground
- one-fourth t. garlic powder
- one-fourth t. smoked paprika

Instructions:

1. Warm up your air fryer to 375°Fahrenheit.
2. In your big dish, toss sweet potatoes, oil, salt, pepper, garlic powder, and paprika.
3. Spread potatoes in your cooking basket and cook for five mins.
4. Shake your basket, then cook for 5 minutes. Shake again and cook for 2 mins until crispy. Serve.

Nutritional Values: Calories: 87; Fat: 3g; Carbs: 13g; Protein: 1g

83. Radish Chips

Prep time: 10 mins | Cook time: 14 mins | Serves: 8

ING:

- 8 large radishes, sliced into chips
- one tbs. olive oil
- half t. sea salt
- one t. curry powder

Instructions:

1. Pat the radish slices dry with a paper towel. Put radishes into your basket and toss with oil plus salt.
2. Warm up your air fryer to 400°Fahrenheit. Cook for 14 mins, tossing once.
3. Sprinkle chips with the curry powder and toss. Serve immediately.

Nutritional Values: Calories: 17; Fat: 2g; Carbs: 1g; Protein: 0g

84. Brie and Bacon Mini Tartlets

Prep time: 10 mins | Cook time: 18 mins | Serves: 6

ING:

- 6 bacon slices
- 16 frozen mini phyllo tartlet shells
- ½ c. diced Brie cheese
- 3 tbs. apple jelly

Instructions:

1. Warm up your air fryer to 400°Fahrenheit. Put bacon in one layer in your basket.
2. Cook for 7 mins, then carefully turn each piece of bacon and cook for 6 mins more.
3. Remove bacon and drain on your paper towels. Crumble when cool and put aside.
4. Discard bacon fat, let basket cool, then wipe it out using your paper towel.
5. Fill tartlet shells with bacon and Brie cubes. Put a bit of apple jelly on top of the filling in each shell.
6. Warm up your air fryer to 350°Fahrenheit. Put filled shells in your basket, then cook for 5 mins. Remove and serve.

Nutritional Values: Calories: 198; Fat: 9g; Carbs: 19g; Protein: 8g

85. Crispy French Fries

Prep time: 5 mins | Cook time: 20 mins | Serves: 4

ING:

- salt, to taste
- three russet potatoes, peeled & sliced into sticks
- two tbs. chopped parsley
- one tbs. olive oil
- two tbs. parmesan cheese

Instructions:

1. Dry the potatoes thoroughly with a paper towel.
2. Mix oil, cheese, parsley, plus salt in your dish. Using this spice combination, coat the French fries.
3. Warm up your air fryer to 360Fahrenheit. Grease your basket using oil and add potatoes.
4. Cook for 10 minutes, toss them, and cook again for 10 minutes. Serve.

Nutritional Values: Calories: 189; Fat: 5g; Carbs: 17g; Protein: 9g

86. Bruschetta Basil Pesto

Prep time: 10 mins | Cook time: 4 mins | Serves: 4

ING:

- eight (half" thick) French bread slices
- two tbs. butter, softened
- one c. mozzarella cheese, shredded
- ½ c. basil pesto
- one c. grape tomatoes, chopped
- two thinly sliced green onions

Instructions:

1. Put butter in your bread slices and move them in your basket. Bake for three mins. Remove your bread and top each using cheese. Bake again for one min.
2. Meanwhile, mix rest of fixings in your small dish. Put bread on your plate, and top each with pesto mixture. Serve.

Nutritional Values: Calories: 462; Fat: 25g; Carbs: 41g; Protein: 19g

87. Air Fryer Popcorn

Prep time: 5 mins | Cook time: 7 mins | Serves: 2

ING:

- ¼ c. popcorn kernels
- Lemon juice, in a spray bottle, for coating
- one t. garlic powder
- two t. nutritional yeast

Instructions:

1. Place the popcorn kernels in your cooking basket, which should be lined on the bottom only with aluminum foil.
2. Grill at 400°F for 7 mins till popcorn stops to pop. Move it to your big dish and lightly mist it using lemon juice. Flavor it using garlic powder and nutritional yeast.
3. Toss to coat all the popcorn. Spray the popcorn again with the lemon juice and toss once more. Serve,

Nutritional Values: Calories: 119; Fat: 1g; Carbs: 25g; Protein: 4g

88. Soda Bread Currant Muffins

Prep time: 15 mins | Cook time: 14 mins | Serves: 6

ING:

- one c. flour, all-purpose
- 2 tbs. flour, whole wheat
- one t. baking powder
- one-eight t. baking soda
- Pinch salt
- 3 tbs. light brown sugar
- half c. dried currants
- one big egg
- ⅓ c. buttermilk
- 3 tbs. butter, melted
- Nonstick baking spray (containing flour)

Instructions:

1. In your med. dish, mix flours, baking powder, baking soda, salt, and sugar. Mix in the currants.
2. In your small dish, mix egg, buttermilk, and melted butter. Combine both mixtures.
3. Spray 6 silicone muffin cups with baking spray. Put batter in between each cup.
4. Warm up your air fryer 350°Fahrenheit. Put muffin cups in your basket. Bake muffins for 14 mins. Serve.

Nutritional Values: Calories: 204; Fat: 7g; Carbs: 32g; Protein: 5g

89. Cheesy Corn Bread

Prep time: 10 mins | Cook time: 17 mins | Serves: 6

ING:

- Nonstick baking spray containing flour
- ⅔ c. yellow cornmeal
- half c. flour, all-purpose
- one t. baking powder
- half t. baking soda
- ¼ t. sea salt
- half c. shredded Cheddar cheese
- one c. buttermilk
- two big eggs
- ¼ c. butter, melted
- 1 tbs. honey

Instructions:

1. Spray a 6-inch round pan with the baking spray. Put aside.
2. Mix cornmeal, flour, baking powder, baking soda, plus salt in your med. dish. Toss in cheese.
3. In your small dish, mix buttermilk, eggs, butter, add honey until smooth. Stir this to your flour mixture. Spread batter into your prepared pan.
4. Warm up your air fryer to 350°Fahrenheit. Bake bread for 17 mins till golden.

Nutritional Values: Calories: 367; Fat: 20g; Carbs: 36g; Protein: 12g

90. Banana-Walnut Bread

Prep time: 10 mins | Cook time: 15 mins | Serves: 4

ING:

- One & ½ c. flour, whole wheat
- One t. baking powder
- One-fourth t. sea salt
- 2 tbs. ground cinnamon
- 2 ripe bananas, mashed
- 3 egg whites
- 2 tbs. applesauce
- One t. pure vanilla extract
- One-fourth c. chopped walnuts
- One-fourth c. dark chocolate chips

Instructions:

1. Warm up your air fryer to 320°Fahrenheit.
2. In your big dish, whisk flour, baking powder, salt, and cinnamon.

3. In another big dish, whisk the mashed bananas, egg whites, applesauce, and vanilla.
4. Combine both mixtures until a smooth dough forms. Fold in walnuts and chocolate chips.
5. Arrange the dough in an air fryer baking dish and add the banana bread. Cook for fifteen mins till golden brown. Serve.

Nutritional Values: Calories: 345; Fat: 10g; Carbs: 59g; Protein: 11g

Chapter 12. DESSERT RECIPES

91. Pound Cake Bites with Cinnamon Dip

Prep time: 10 mins | Cook time: 3 mins | Serves: 6

ING:

- one (16-ounce) frozen pound cake, thawed, cubed
- ⅓ c. sugar
- 1½ t. ground cinnamon, divided
- 4 tbs. butter, melted
- 1 c. vanilla Greek yogurt
- 3 tbs. packed light brown sugar
- ½ t. vanilla extract

Instructions:

1. In your shallow dish, mix sugar and one teaspoon cinnamon.
2. Drizzle cake cubes with the melted butter, then toss them in the shallow bowl with the sugar mixture.
3. Warm up your air fryer to 350°Fahrenheit. Put cake cubes in one layer in your basket.
4. Cook the cubes for 3 mins or until golden. Remove the cake cubes and put on your serving plate. Repeat with a second batch.
5. Meanwhile, in your small dish, mix yogurt, sugar, remaining cinnamon, plus vanilla. When all cake cubes are done, serve them with the dip.

Nutritional Values: Calories: 425; Fat: 18g; Carbs: 61g; Protein: 6g

92. Chocolate Chunk Cookies

Prep time: 10 mins | Cook time: 5 mins | Serves: 12 cookies

ING:

- 8 tbs. unsalted butter
- half c. coconut sugar
- one tbs. molasses
- one egg
- one t. vanilla extract
- one c. whole-wheat flour
- half t. baking soda
- one-fourth t. salt
- half c. dark chocolate chunks

Instructions:

1. Warm up your air fryer to 350°Fahrenheit. Prepare your basket using baking paper.

2. In your big dish, using your electric mixer, beat butter, coconut sugar, plus molasses, speed until fluffy. Beat in egg and vanilla.
3. Beat in flour, baking soda, and salt. Mix in the chocolate chunks. Split your dough into 12 and put each on your parchment paper. Bake for 5 mins. Serve.

Nutritional Values: Calories: 369; Fat: 22g; Carbs: 40g; Protein: 5g

93. Grilled Curried Fruit

Prep time: 10 mins | Cook time: 5 mins | Serves: 6

ING:

- 2 peaches, pitted & sliced into wedges
- 2 firm pears, halved, stemmed, cored & sliced into wedges
- 2 plums, halved, stemmed, cored & sliced into wedges
- 2 tbs. melted butter
- 1 tbs. honey
- 2 to 3 t. curry powder

Instructions:

1. Spread a large sheet of heavy-duty foil on your work surface. Arrange the fruit on the foil and drizzle using butter and honey. Flavor it using curry powder.
2. Wrap the fruit in the foil, making sure to leave some air space in the packet.
3. Put the foil packet in the basket, then grill for 5 mins, shaking once, until the fruit is soft and tender.

Nutritional Values: Calories: 107; Fat: 4g; Carbs: 19g; Protein: 1g

94. Pistachio Baked Pears

Prep time: 10 mins | Cook time: 11 mins | Serves: 4

ING:

- two big ripe pears, halved & pitted
- two tbs. butter, dissolved
- three tbs. brown sugar
- ⅛ t. cinnamon
- ½ c. whole unsalted shelled pistachios
- Pinch sea salt

Instructions:

1. Put the pears into the air fryer basket, cut side up. Brush pears using butter, then sprinkle using sugar and cinnamon.
2. Warm up your air fryer to 350°Fahrenheit. Bake for 8 mins.
3. Sprinkle the pears using pistachios, concentrating them in the hollow where the seeds were. Flavor it using salt.
4. Bake for another 3 minutes till pears are tender. Serve.

Nutritional Values: Calories: 180; Fat: 9g; Carbs: 25g; Protein: 2g

95. Cracker Candy

Prep time: 10 mins | Cook time: 10 mins | Serves: 4

ING:

- Nonstick cooking spray
- 10 to 12 round buttery crackers
- 4 tbs. butter
- ¼ c. packed light brown sugar
- ½ c. milk chocolate chips
- ¼ c. chopped cashews

Instructions:

1. Line a 7-by-2-inch round baking pan using foil, then coat it using oil spray.
2. Line bottom with the crackers, breaking some crackers to fill the gaps.
3. In your small pan, mix butter and sugar. Boil over moderate temp, stirring constantly. Boil within 1 minute. Pour it over your pan.
4. Warm up your air fryer to 375°Fahrenheit. Bake candy for 3 mins. Remove your pan, then sprinkle using chocolate chips.
5. Allow to stand for a few minutes, then swirl the chocolate over the candy.
6. Sprinkle with the cashews and let stand until cool. Remove from the pan and break into pieces to serve.

Nutritional Values: Calories: 364; Fat: 24g; Carbs: 35g; Protein: 3g

96. Apple Peach Cranberry Crisp

Prep time: 10 mins | Cook time: 10 mins | Serves: 8

ING:

- one apple, peeled & chopped
- two peaches, peeled & chopped
- ⅓ c. dried cranberries
- two tbs. honey
- ⅓ c. brown sugar
- ¼ c. flour
- ½ c. oatmeal
- 3 tbs. softened butter

Instructions:

1. In your 6-x-6-x-2" pan, mix apple, peaches, cranberries, and honey.
2. In your medium dish, combine the sugar, flour, oatmeal, plus butter until crumbly. Put this mixture over your fruit.
3. Bake for 10 mins till topping is golden brown. Serve.

Nutritional Values: Calories: 134; Fat: 5g; Carbs: 23g; Protein: 1g

97. Peanut Butter Brownies

Prep time: 10 mins | Cook time: 13 mins | Serves: 8

ING:

- ½ c. brown sugar
- ¼ c. peanut butter
- 3 tbs. butter, melted
- one big egg
- one t. vanilla
- one-third cup flour, all-purpose
- one-eight t. baking powder
- Pinch sea salt
- Nonstick baking spray containing flour
- 3 tbs. chopped salted peanuts

Instructions:

1. In your medium dish, mix sugar, peanut butter, and butter. Beat in egg and vanilla and beat.
2. Mix in the flour, baking powder and salt until combined.
3. Grease your 6" round dish using the baking spray. Spread batter into the dish. Sprinkle with the peanuts.
4. Warm up your air fryer to 325°Fahrenheit. Bake for 13 mins till brownies look set. Serve.

Nutritional Values: Calories: 169; Fat: 11g; Carbs: 15g; Protein: 4g

98. Carrot Cake Muffins

Prep time: 10 mins | Cook time: 15 mins | Serves: 6

ING:

- one c. grated carrot
- ⅓ c. chopped pineapple
- ¼ c. raisins
- 2 tbs. pure maple syrup
- ⅓ c. unsweetened milk
- one c. oat flour
- one t. ground cinnamon
- half t. ground ginger
- one t. baking powder
- ½ t. baking soda

- One-third c. chopped walnuts

Instructions:

1. In your medium dish, mix carrot, pineapple, raisins, maple syrup, and milk.
2. Mix in oat flour, cinnamon, ginger, baking powder, and baking soda.
3. Divide the batter evenly among 6 cupcake molds. Then sprinkle the chopped walnuts evenly over each muffin.
4. Lightly press the walnuts into the batter so they are partially submerged. Bake in your air fryer at 350°Fahrenheit for 15 mins.

Nutritional Values: Calories: 170; Fat: 6g; Carbs: 27g; Protein: 4g

99. Mini Baked Apple Pies

Prep time: 10 mins | Cook time: 10 mins | Serves: 4

ING:

- 2 Granny Smith apples, peeled & diced
- 1 tbs. unsalted butter, melted
- 2½ tbs. evaporated cane sugar, divided
- ½ t. ground cinnamon
- ⅛ t. ground nutmeg
- 1 tbs. lemon juice
- 4 t. water, divided
- ½ c. plain Greek yogurt
- ½ c. whole-wheat flour, plus more for dusting
- 1 egg

Instructions:

1. Warm up your air fryer to 350°F.
2. In your big dish, mix apples, butter, two tbsp sugar, the cinnamon, nutmeg, lemon juice, and 3 tsp water. Put aside.
3. In your medium dish, mix yogurt, rest of sugar, and flour until a sticky dough forms.
4. Divide your dough into 4. Dust your clean work surface using flour and put each dough into a 4" circle.
5. In your small dish, whisk egg plus remaining water for egg wash.
6. Divide apple mixture between four 6-ounce ramekins. Top each ramekin with a dough circle. Brush the tops using egg wash.
7. Put ramekins in your cooking basket and cook for 10 mins. Serve immediately.

Nutritional Values: Calories: 195; Fat: 6g; Carbs: 32g; Protein: 5g

100. Chewy Date Bars

Prep time: 10 mins | Cook time: 10 mins | Serves: 4 bars

ING:

- ½ c. raw cashews
- ¼ c. unsalted natural peanut butter
- ½ c. rolled oats
- two tbs. chia seeds
- 5 Medjool dates, pitted
- 2 tbs. almond milk
- one t. cinnamon, ground
- half t. nutmeg, ground
- one-fourth t. cloves, ground
- one-fourth t. sea salt

Instructions:

1. In a high-speed blender, combine the cashews, peanut butter, oats, chia, dates, milk, cinnamon, nutmeg, cloves, and salt.
2. Pulse on high speed until the dough starts to come together. Prepare your cooking basket using parchment paper.
3. Pour the batter into the bottom, pressing it firmly down with your fingers to form an even layer.
4. Warm up your air fryer to 320°Fahrenheit and cook for 8 mins, until golden brown on top. Slice into bars and serve.

Nutritional Values: Calories: 337; Fat: 18g; Carbs: 41g; Protein: 9g

RECIPE INDEX

A

Air Fryer Lamb Meatballs	36
Air Fryer Popcorn	62
Apple Peach Cranberry Crisp	67
Apricots in Blankets	55

B

Baked Chili-Lime Tilapia	39
Baked Eggs in Tomato Sauce	15
Balsamic Roasted Chicken Thighs	24
Banana-Walnut Bread	63
Beef Tips and Gravy	30
Breaded Turkey Cutlets	28
Breakfast Monkey Bread	14
Brie and Bacon Mini Tartlets	60
Bruschetta Basil Pesto	61
Buffalo Cauliflower Bites	56

C

Cajun-Spiced Roasted Pecans	59
California Fish Tacos	37
Caramelized Sweet Potatoes	46
Carrot Cake Muffins	68
Cheesy Corn Bread	63
Chewy Date Bars	70
Chicken Casserole	23
Chicken Fajitas	20
Chicken Parm Hoagies	22
Chicken Satay	24
Chili-Lime Bean and Rice Burritos	48
Chocolate Chunk Cookies	65
Cilantro Butter Baked Mahi Mahi	37
Cottage Cheesy Pancakes	13
Cracker Candy	67
Cranberry Oatmeal Muffins	17
Cranberry Turkey Quesadillas	26
Crispy Calamari	42
Crispy French Fries	61
Crispy Fried Okra	51

Crispy Ginger Edamame 52
Crispy Mushrooms 44
Crispy Sweet Potato Fries 59
Crustless Mini Quiches..14
Curried Chicken Nuggets 20

F

Five-Spice Broccoli 46

G

Garlic-Dill Salmon with Tomatoes..39
Garlic-Herb Rib Eye...31
Garlicky Green Beans 49
Grilled Curried Fruit...66

H

Herbed Lamb Steaks...35
Herbed Vegetable Breakfast Bake 15
Herbed Vegetable Mélange 51
Honey-Balsamic Salmon...38
Honey-Garlic Pork Chops..32

I

Italian Frittata 11

J

Jalapeño Poppers 54

L

Lemon Pork Tenderloin...34
Lemon-Herb Tuna Steaks 40
Lemony Sea Scallops 41

M

Mini Baked Apple Pies 69
Mini Turkey Meatloaves 25
Mongolian Beef..29
Mushroom Scrambled Eggs 11

Mustard Lamb Chops 34

N

Nut and Berry Granola 13
Nutty French Toast..12

O

Orange Chicken and Snap Peas 21

P

Parmesan Asparagus 45
Parmesan Garlic Shrimp...41
Peaches and Cream Oatmeal Bake..18
Peanut Butter Brownies..68
Pesto Omelet 16
Pistachio Baked Pears...66
Pork Belly Bites 31
Pork Medallions in Mustard Sauce..33
Pound Cake Bites with Cinnamon Dip 65

R

Radish Chips...60
Raspberry-Stuffed French Toast..17
Roasted Carrots...45
Roasted Cherry Tomatoes 52
Roasted Garlic and Onion Dip...57
Roasted Garlic Brussels Sprouts..48
Roasted Italian Bell Peppers...47
Roasted Spicy Corn 44
Roasted Waldorf Salad..50
Rosemary Lamb Chops 36

S

Sage and Pear Sausage Patties...12
Savory Lamb Chops..35
Shrimp and Crab Cakes..42
Soda Bread Currant Muffins 62
Spinach-Cranberry Turnovers..54
Sriracha Tuna Melt..38
Steak Bites and Mushrooms 29

Steamed Green Veggie Trio 49
Stir-Fried Chicken with Pineapple...22
Stir-Fried Steak and Cabbage 30
Stir-Fried Zucchini and Yellow Squash 50
Sweet-and-Sour Polish Sausage...32

T

Tandoori-Style Chickpeas 57
Tex-Mex Cheese Sticks 56
Tex-Mex Turkey Burgers...25
Tofu Scramble Bowls 18
Turkey Spinach Meatballs 26
Turkey-Stuffed Bell Peppers..27
Turkey–Stuffed Zucchini Boats 27

AIR FRYER TIME TABLE

This is a general chart for reference. Your air fryer may have different cooking times and temperatures; follow the instructions that came with your appliance.

VEGETABLES			
French fries (thin, frozen)	2 to 4 cups	390°F	10 to 14 minutes
If you find ice on the fries, remove it; toss once during cooking.			
French fries (thin, fresh)	2 to 4 cups	400°F	15 to 20 minutes
Pat dry; toss with cornstarch and ½ teaspoon sugar for better browning, then mist with oil; toss once during cooking.			
French fries (thick, frozen)	2 to 4 cups	380°F	12 to 20 minutes
If you find ice on the fries, remove it.			
French fries (thick, fresh)	2 to 4 cups	400°F	15 to 25 minutes
Lightly spray with oil.			
Potato wedges	2 to 4 cups	390°F	18 to 22 minutes
Lightly spray with oil; sprinkle with salt and pepper.			

Chips	3 to 7 cups	400°F	7 to 12 minutes
Toss once or twice during cooking.			
Chopped potatoes	4 to 7 cups	400°F	13 to 19 minutes
Spray with oil; toss once or twice during cooking.			
Potato slices	4 to 5 cups	380°F	10 to 15 minutes
Slice about ⅛" thick; spray with oil; toss during cooking.			
Cauliflower florets	2 to 4 cups	390°F	5 to 9 minutes
Mist with oil and season before frying; toss once during cooking.			
Other Vegetables	1 to 3 pounds	350°F	Sliced eggplant: 15 to 20 minutes Zucchini: 10 minutes Onions: 4 to 7 minutes Tomatoes: Whole for 8 minutes, Slices for 4 minutes Green beans: Whole for 5 to 7 minutes
Cook vegetables individually. • Sliced onions work better than chopped. • Cut to similar sizes. • Toss once during cooking.			

POULTRY AND MEAT			
Chicken nuggets	1 to 4 cups	370°F	7 to 12 minutes
If you find ice on the chicken, remove it.			
Chicken wings	1 to 3 pounds	380°F	15 to 20 minutes
Cook to an internal temperature of 165°F; toss once during cooking.			
Chicken drumsticks	1 to 6 drumsticks	400°F and 320°F	8 minutes at 400°F, then 10 to 12 minutes at 320°F
Pat dry; do not rinse. Spray with oil and sprinkle with seasonings.			
Chicken breast	1 to 6 6-ounce boneless, skinless halves	360°F	10 to 16 minutes
Place in a single layer in the basket; turn once during cooking.			
Pork chops	1 to 4 1" thick chops	350°F	7 to 10 minutes
Cook to a minimum internal temperature of 145°F. Place in a single layer; turn once during cooking (optional).			
Burgers	1 to 4 4-ounce patties	360°F	6 to 9 minutes
Place in single layer; turn once during cooking. Cook to a minimum internal temperature of 160°F.			
Frozen meatballs	25 per batch	380°F	6 to 8 minutes
If you find ice on the meatballs, remove it.			

Raw meatballs	25 per batch	390°F	6 to 9 minutes
	Don't crowd; place in a single layer in the basket; turn with tongs halfway through cooking time.		
Steak	1 to 4 6-ounce steaks, ¾ inch thick	360°F	8 to 12 minutes
	Time depends on desired doneness; use a food thermometer to cook to 140°F for medium rare; 160°F for well done.		

FISH

Fish sticks (frozen)	1 to 3 cups	390°F	8 to 10 minutes
	If you find ice on the fish, remove it.		
Shrimp (frozen)	1 to 2 pounds	390°F	8 minutes
	If you find ice on the shrimp, remove it; can bread before cooking.		
Shrimp (fresh)	1 to 2 pounds	390°F	5 minutes
	Shell and devein shrimp; pat dry. Can bread before cooking.		
Salmon fillets	4 6-ounce fillets	300°F	9 to 14 minutes
	Brush with oil and sprinkle with seasonings before cooking to an internal temperature of 140°F.		
Salmon steak	4 8-ounce steaks	300°F	14 to 18 minutes
	Brush with oil and sprinkle with seasonings; cook to an internal temperature of 140°F.		

OTHER			
Egg rolls	6 to 8	390°F	3 to 6 minutes
Brush or mist with oil before cooking.			
Pizza	1 pizza	390°F	5 to 10 minutes
Place pizza on parchment paper in the basket. Make sure it fits into the basket.			
Grilled cheese sandwiches	1 to 3 sandwiches	400°F	7 minutes
Place on parchment paper; turn with tongs halfway through cooking.			
Cake	1 8-inch pan	320°F	20 to 25 minutes
Use a cake pan that fits easily inside the basket.			
Muffins	10 muffins	360°F	10 to 12 minutes
Muffins should be placed inside double foil cups; place in single layer.			
Fruit	2 to 4 cups	320°F	3 to 5 minutes for soft fruits; 5 to 10 minutes for hard fruits
Cook hard fruits, such as apples, and soft fruits, such as peaches, separately.			

COOKING CONVERSION CHART

Volume Equivalents (Liquid)

US STANDARD	US STANDARD (OUNCES)	METRIC (APPROXIMATE)
2 tablespoons	1 fl. oz.	30 mL
¼ cup	2 fl. oz.	60 mL
½ cup	4 fl. oz.	120 mL
1 cup	8 fl. oz.	240 mL
1½ cups	12 fl. oz.	355 mL
2 cups or 1 pint	16 fl. oz.	475 mL
4 cups or 1 quart	32 fl. oz.	1 L
1 gallon	128 fl. oz.	4 L

Volume Equivalents (Dry)

US STANDARD	METRIC (APPROXIMATE)
⅛ teaspoon	0.5 mL
¼ teaspoon	1 mL
½ teaspoon	2 mL
¾ teaspoon	4 mL
1 teaspoon	5 mL
1 tablespoon	15 mL
¼ cup	59 mL
⅓ cup	79 mL
½ cup	118 mL
⅔ cup	156 mL
¾ cup	177 mL
1 cup	235 mL
2 cups or 1 pint	475 mL
3 cups	700 mL
4 cups or 1 quart	1 L
½ gallon	2 L
1 gallon	4 L

Oven Temperatures

FAHRENHEIT (F)	CELSIUS (C) (APPROXIMATE)
250	120
300	150
325	165
350	180
375	190
400	200
425	220
450	230

Weight Equivalents

US STANDARD	METRIC (APPROXIMATE)
½ ounce	15 g
1 ounce	30 g
2 ounces	60 g
4 ounces	115 g
8 ounces	225 g
12 ounces	340 g
16 ounces or 1 pound	455 g

Conclusion

In this cookbook, we have strived to make air frying easy and accessible to beginners. We understand that learning how to cook with an air fryer can seem intimidating at first, but we hope that this guide has made the process smoother for you. Whether you're grilling, roasting, or baking, there's something in here for everyone. The recipes we've included are not only quick and easy but also healthy and delicious.

We hope that as you've worked your way through this cookbook, you've discovered a new passion for cooking and experimenting with new ingredients and flavors. Don't be afraid to put your own spin on the recipes we've provided, and don't hesitate to share your own unique dishes with family and friends. Air frying is a versatile and healthy way of cooking, and we hope that our recipes have inspired you to try out new dishes beyond what's been included in this book. Remember to always keep your air fryer clean and follow the manufacturer's instructions for cooking times and temperatures. With the right ingredients, a little creativity, and an air fryer, the possibilities are truly endless. With an air fryer, you can indulge in juicy roasts, crisp yet healthy veggie dishes, and guilt-free desserts! So, why limit yourself to a traditional oven or a fryer that tends to soak your food in unwholesome oil? Whether you're seeking a quick fix after a long day at work or preparing for a big dinner party, an air fryer is a versatile and efficient tool that can do it all.